10-Minute Tarot

10-Minute Tarot

Read the Future in an Instant

Skye Alexander

FAIR WINDS
PRESS
GLOUCESTER, MASSACHUSETTS

Text © 2003 by Skye Alexander

First published in the USA in 2003 by

Fair Winds Press

33 Commercial Street

Gloucester, MA 01930

Library of Congress Cataloging-in-Publication Data available

ISBN 1-59233-018-5

10 9 8 7 6 5 4 3 2

Cover design by Laura Shaw Design

Book design by Anne Gram

Printed and bound in Canada

To my friends,
who together form a living tarot to guide me
on my journey.

Contents

Introduction

No one knows exactly where or when the tarot (pro-
nounced *tah-ROH*) originated. It may have derived from
ancient Egyptian tablets engraved with hieroglyphics or
from the Chaldeans' secret texts. Some researchers believe
the Knights Templar brought the tarot back to Europe with
them after the Crusades. Others trace its roots to the gypsies
who traveled through the continent during the Middle
Ages. Evidence suggests that seventy-eight-card tarot decks
much like the ones we're familiar with might have been
used to tell fortunes in Italy and France during the
Renaissance. Our present-day playing cards may have
evolved from these early tarot decks.

What we do know is that the tarot has survived for seven hundred years as one of the Western world's most important bodies of mystical knowledge. More than a device for divination, it provides a key to understanding universal truths and shows the way to enlightenment. In recent years, its popularity has grown steadily, and today the tarot is our most-used form of divination.

The tarot continues to be a living, evolving medium. "The Tarot cards are not a single system, or a discrete philosophy, or a single truth. . . . There are instead many Tarots," says Brian Williams, creator of the Minchiate Tarot.

How to Use This Book

It takes years of study and practice to become adept at reading the tarot. Like most bodies of esoteric knowledge, it probably can never be fully understood. But you don't have to be an expert to benefit from the wisdom of the tarot.

10-Minute Tarot doesn't pretend to be an in-depth study of this complex oracle. This book is designed for practical, busy people who want to learn the fundamentals so they can use the tarot to guide them in their daily lives.

Part One covers the basics of the tarot, how it works, and how to use it successfully. A number of "spreads," or patterns, for doing card readings are provided in the section, too. I also explain a bit about oracles in general and the art of divination.

Part Two gives quick and easy to comprehend interpretations of each card in a standard tarot deck. I've provided four or five meanings for each of the seventy-eight cards, based on the subject being considered. That's because you interpret a card somewhat differently when asking a question about love than when seeking advice about a financial matter.

Tarot cards can also serve as subjects for meditation and contemplation. Select a card randomly from the deck or intentionally choose one that represents something you are working on in your own life. Reflecting upon Strength, for example, can help you develop resilience, perseverance, and the power to overcome obstacles.

10-Minute Tarot lets beginners start using the tarot right away. Turn to the interpretations in Part Two to find answers to questions, gain insight into yourself and others, or see what the future holds. Hopefully, even knowledge-able tarot enthusiasts will find something of value here, for each of us brings our own perceptions and experiences to the study of this venerable oracle.

Part One, Chapter 1
Oracles

During times of transformation, when we must face challenges, make decisions, or change our familiar ways of doing things, oracles can serve as road maps on the journey into unknown territory. Sometimes they are our only guides. The tarot, runes, *I Ching,* astrology, and other divination aids shine light into the darkness to help us see where we are going.

Since ancient times, people in cultures around the world have consulted oracles in an attempt to see into the future. The three-thousand-year-old *I Ching* is believed to have evolved from an even older Chinese divination method of interpreting cracks in tortoise shells. The Apache watched muscles twitching in a person's body to determine whether good or evil lay ahead. People in the deserts of Northern Africa and the Middle East read the future in sand patterns.

Divination, the art of predicting or "divining" the future, literally means to let the divine realm manifest. Oracles are devices (or sages, like the Oracle at Delphi) through which the deities speak. They help us understand the forces operating beneath the surface of a situation to reveal angles we might not have been aware of otherwise, so we can see problems more accurately. They suggest ways to handle challenges and opportunities. They caution or encourage us. Their advice may be ambiguous at times, but they never lie.

As I explain in my book *10-Minute Crystal Ball,* the tarot and other oracles "operate on the premise that the answers to all questions already exist and that some part of you—your subconscious, higher mind, inner wisdom, or whatever you choose to call it—knows the answers. The trick is to access the information and bring it into your awareness. Through symbols, colors, meaningful patterns, movement, and imagery, oracles help you bypass your rational, logical intellect and its limited understanding so you can see the big picture."

An Elegant Oracle

The tarot serves as a direct link—a cosmic conference call, so to speak—between your conscious self, your subconscious, and Divine Wisdom. *Cartomancy,* the art of divination by cards, is based on two principles: Each moment embodies a unique quality, and everything in the Universe—unseen as well as seen—is connected. When we shuffle tarot cards (or use any other oracle), we open our consciousness to perceive the essence of that moment.

The most elegant of all oracles, the tarot's illustrated cards can be configured in dozens of patterns to provide in-depth information about virtually any matter or situation.

Although it would be foolish to suggest that one oracle is better than another, the tarot is certainly more colorful than the *I Ching*, and its seventy-eight cards offer greater depth, subtlety, and diversity than the twenty-five letters in a standard set of runes. It's also more portable than the equipment needed to calculate astrology charts.

Many of today's most popular decks, including the Rider-Waite deck and Crowley's Thoth Tarot, were developed during the first half of the twentieth century. Another wave of interest in the 1970s led to the creation of specialized tarot decks such as the round Motherpeace deck, as well as a revival of some early designs. In recent years, scores of artists have interpreted the tarot to reflect a wide range of cultures, philosophies, and spiritual paths.

The tarot isn't static. It is a living oracle and continues to evolve as an art form, a predictive tool, and a means for understanding ourselves and our world.

Choosing a Tarot Deck

Choosing a tarot deck is a purely personal decision. No deck is "better" or more authentic than any other. The Rider-Waite deck, created by Arthur Edward Waite and Pamela Coleman Smith, is the most popular deck today, and many books on the tarot refer to it, but that doesn't mean it's the right one for you. Because I'm an Art Deco fan, I like the Aquarian Tarot. The Sacred Circle Tarot, which appeals to my Celtic Pagan worldview, is another of my favorites. (I don't recommend the beautiful, fifteenth-century Visconti deck for beginners, however, because the major arcana cards aren't labeled and can be tricky to identify.)

So many unique and interesting tarot decks are now available that there's something for everyone. You'll find American Indian decks, Egyptian decks, Irish, Chinese, Russian, German, and Japanese decks, feng shui decks, angel decks, goddess, fairy, dragon, unicorn, crystal, cat, erotic, and herbal decks—you can even buy one that glows in the dark. People who prefer an electronic oracle might enjoy Visionary Software's Tarot Magic CD-ROM, which includes ten different tarot decks and a number of spread options for doing computerized interactive readings.

Tarot decks come in various sizes, and although most are rectangular, the popular Motherpeace deck is round. Some decks feature oversized cards that are hard to shuffle in the usual manner, but many people like these because the graphics are larger. Miniature decks are convenient to carry, but I find them difficult to use.

Purchasing a tarot deck is literally a hands-on experience. Many stores that sell tarot decks display samples so you can see and handle the cards before you buy them. Some big chain stores have catalogs of decks. Stuart Kaplan's three-volume *Encyclopedia of the Tarot* contains photos and descriptions of hundreds of decks. U.S. Games

Systems distributes a huge number of decks—you may want to visit their Web site at www.usgamesinc.com to see what's available.

Tarot decks are like tattoos—one isn't always enough. Many people collect decks. Some like to keep several different decks to use depending on their mood. Those of us who do readings often have one deck for ourselves and one for clients. You may want a deck to use for readings and another for meditation or magical purposes.

I use three tarot decks on a regular basis and own more than two dozen culled from about a hundred that have passed through my hands over the years. I'm also in the process of creating my own deck. The profound concepts put forth in the tarot offer a wealth of inspiration and challenges for many artists, including the notorious surrealistic painter Salvador Dalí. Dalí's wife, Gala, encouraged his interest in mysticism, and he created his beautiful deck for her.

Caring for Your Cards

Tarot cards are extremely sensitive—they pick up and respond to the subtle energies of anyone who touches them. It's a good idea to clear or "smudge" a new deck of cards before using them. One of the simplest ways to do this is to light a sage smudge wand or stick of incense and hold the deck in the smoke for a minute or so. Close your eyes and envision white light surrounding and purifying the cards. When I do readings for other people, I like to cleanse the cards between users to remove traces of each person's energy so it doesn't influence the next person's reading.

Vibrations in the environment can also affect your cards. To protect them from ambient energies as well as from dust and smoke, store them in a pouch, box, or other container. Some people like to wrap them in a piece of silk cloth.

Over time, your tarot deck will become a trusted friend and confidant—treat it as such. Show the cards the respect and confidant—treat it as such. Show the cards the respect you'd give to a human counselor, teacher, or guide. After receiving advice, thank them (and the source behind the wisdom they imparted) for their help. The more you work with the tarot, the more it will reveal its secrets to you.

Chapter 2

The Major and Minor Arcana

The tarot is composed of two parts known as the minor arcana and the major arcana. (*Arcana* means mysterious knowledge.) Early tarot decks may have contained only the twenty-two cards in the major arcana. Some tarot scholars believe the minor arcana evolved from a game played in Europe during the Middle Ages and was added to the major arcana at a later date. The minor arcana is similar to our contemporary playing cards of four suits, each containing ten numbered cards and four court cards—in fact, poker decks may have descended from the tarot's minor arcana.

The Major Arcana

The major arcana is an illustrated course in self-development, a journey from innocence to enlightenment. Beginning with The Fool, this symbolic sojourn takes the seeker through twenty-two steps of initiation to mastery and wholeness, culminating with The World. Each card represents a stage of growth, building on the insights of the previous card and leading to the discoveries of the following one. For instance, the confusion and mystery characterized by The Moon (card #18) evolve into a state of clarity depicted by The Sun (#19).

The cards in the major arcana describe "fated" or "cosmic" conditions, with implications that extend beyond personal or mundane situations. When many major arcana or "trump" cards turn up in a reading, it can mean that you are being influenced by circumstances and forces outside your control. Major arcana cards also represent spiritual dimensions and archetypes, as well as experiences that shape us on an inner level, whether or not they manifest in the outer world.

Although most tarot decks contain fundamental similarities, artistic license allows for many individual depictions. Not all decks use the same numbering or names for the major arcana cards. Some decks switch the order of Strength and Justice, for instance. Some add one or more cards—even blank ones so the user can create a uniquely personal tarot. Some refer to The Hierophant as Jupiter, The High Priest, or The Pope; many label The World The Universe. One of the most popular decks, Aleister Crowley's Thoth Tarot, replaces the Strength card with Lust, Justice with Adjustment, Temperance with Art, and Judgment with Aeon. Some, such as the Shapeshifter Tarot, take a great deal of liberty and rename most of the cards.

Usually, the major arcana includes twenty-two cards. In Part Two, I interpret these cards in greater detail, but their basic meanings are:

The Fool = innocence, beginnings, trust

The Magician = hidden powers, working behind the scenes

The High Priestess = intuition, emotions

The Empress = mature female, self-esteem, mastery

The Emperor = mature male, organization, pragmatism

The Hierophant = leadership, higher knowledge, structure

The Lovers = union of opposites, relationships, choices

The Chariot = mysterious forces at work, harnessing power

Strength = overcoming weaknesses, inner power

The Hermit = retreat, reflection, self-reliance

The Wheel of Fortune = a change for the better, good luck

Justice = trial, equality, honesty, rectification

The Hanged Man = relinquishing control, letting go, sacrifice

Death = transformation, loss and rebirth

Temperance = moderation, balance, acceptance

The Devil = obsession, fear, materialism

The Tower = change, destruction of the old resulting in freedom

The Star = hope, ideals, happiness, success

The Moon = illusion, secrets, the subconscious, mystery

The Sun = clarity, contentment, self-expression

Judgment = choices, change, regeneration

The World = progress, order and harmony, achievement

The Minor Arcana

The minor arcana usually contains fifty-six cards, although some decks deviate from this standard. The Minchiate Tarot, for instance, has sixteen additional cards that represent astrological factors. Cards in this part of the tarot describe everyday matters, experiences, and events over which you have control. According to A. T. Mann in the *Elements of the Tarot,* "the minor arcana cards represent the outer manifestations of the archetypal principles embodied in the major arcana cards."

The minor arcana is divided into four suits—wands, pentacles, cups, and swords. The suit of wands relates to creativity and inspiration; pentacles correspond to money and physical matters; cups deal with emotions and relationships; swords are linked with communication and ideas. The tarot's connection with astrology is clearly demonstrated in the suits, which represent the four elements: wands = fire, pentacles = earth, cups = water, and swords = air. The suits also symbolize the four levels of being: wands = spirit, pentacles = body, cups = emotion, and swords = mind. Magical practitioners will also notice that the four suits depict the four primary tools in a magician's toolbox (see my book *10-Minute Magic Spells* for more information). In a regular poker deck, wands correspond to clubs, pentacles to diamonds, cups to hearts, and swords to spades.

Many tarot decks depict the suit of swords in negative terms, and some of the imagery can be quite scary. I suspect this may be because analytical thought is a left-brain function and contradictory to the intuitive, right-brain manner in which the tarot conveys knowledge. The ten of swords, for instance, often shows a person with ten swords piercing his or her back, which at first glance could indicate treachery, betrayal, and suffering. If, however, you look at ten as the number of maximum development and swords as mental activity, you can see that this card usually means you've been worrying about something so much you've reached a point of exhaustion—I call it the "give it a rest" card. It can also suggest learning a lesson the hard way, or as the Austrian mystic Rudolf Steiner said, "Wisdom is crystallized pain." In my opinion, no suit is inherently "bad"—all four contain cards that represent difficulties, unhappiness, or unpleasant circumstances, as well as cards connoting victory, success, and hope.

Typically, each suit in the minor arcana contains fourteen cards, ten numbered or "pip" cards (ace through ten) and four court cards. The ace signifies the initial stages of a matter. Numbered cards describe development on a theme, leading up to the ten, which shows fulfillment or completion.

Variations in the minor arcana as well as the major arcana occur from deck to deck. Some decks refer to wands as rods or staves; pentacles may be labeled coins or discs; cups are sometimes called chalices; swords may turn up as daggers. The Wheel of Change Tarot depicts the suits in many unusual ways—jagged pieces of glass represent swords, drums and spider webs stand in for pentacles. The Animal-Wise Tarot links animals with the suits. Decks with distinct ethnic or spiritual connections may use special terminology, such as the Gaelic words and ogham letters that appear on the Faery Wicca Tarot cards. Regardless of what names they go by, the energies and conditions the cards symbolize remain pretty much the same.

Early pip cards featured pictures of the objects associated with the suits but did not include people or scenes, as many modern tarot decks do. Storytelling images were added to the basic symbolism of the minor arcana in the first half of the twentieth century. These images can be helpful to beginners, for they describe the essence of the cards' meanings in visual terms. They also trigger insights and impressions that can lead to deeper understanding.

Court Cards

Most decks include four court cards per suit in the minor arcana. Court cards may symbolize actual people or principles at work. The princess of cups, for example, could represent your sensitive adolescent daughter or your own immature emotional responses that stem from childhood experiences.

Generally speaking, kings symbolize mature men, strength, leadership, and mastery in areas related to the suit. Queens signify mature women, creative power, depth, and confidence in areas related to the suit. Kings show a "masculine" way of utilizing the energies, through assertiveness, outward or physical activity, or left-brain reasoning; queens describe a "feminine" way of expressing energies, through nurturing, imagination, inner strength, or right-brain functioning.

Knights or princes can represent younger male figures or undeveloped energies related to the suit. They usually show an active approach to a situation, but one that is indecisive, undependable, or unstable. Knights are associated with quests—physical, mental, emotional, or spiritual—and in some instances these court cards indicate travel or movement. Pages or princesses can denote younger female figures, apprentices/students, people in support positions, or an immature expression of the suit. These cards signify naïveté, learning, seeking, or a need for self-development. Sometimes they refer to messages or messengers.

Even though court cards depict male and female figures, they needn't be interpreted as gender-specific when describing real people. Rather, these cards indicate character traits, personality, or *modus operandi*. A strong, pragmatic woman who heads a business could be represented by the king of pentacles, whereas the queen of cups could stand for a sensitive, artistic man.

The terminology used varies from deck to deck. Some include princes and princesses in the court cards, others label these cards knights or knaves and pages. Specialized decks may use other terms, such as god and goddess, lord and lady, mother and father, seeker, warrior, and so on.

Numerology and the Tarot

The esoteric art of numerology, which holds that numbers are symbols that describe energies and cycles, plays an important role in the tarot. You'll notice that the cards in both the major and minor arcana are numbered. Some people associate the even numbers with "good" or easy conditions and the odd numbers with "bad" or difficult situations. I think it's more accurate to say that the even numbers tend to indicate stability, while the odd ones show change or movement. The basic meanings of the numbers are as follows:

1 (ace) = beginnings, focused energy

2 = partnerships, polarity, duality, seeking balance

3 = development, synthesis, productivity, completion of a phase

4 = solidification, stability, rigidity

5 = dispersion, instability, challenge, change

6 = give-and-take, intersection, cooperation, balance

7 = individual approaches and expression

8 = intensification of energy, establishment, seriousness

9 = expansion, increase

10 = achievement, fullness, maximum development

Numbers must be interpreted in conjunction with the suit involved. The ace of pentacles, for example, could mean a new job, whereas the ace of cups might indicate the start of a love affair.

Numbers can also signify cycles or phases. A tarot spread that contains many low-numbered cards shows that a matter is in the early stages of development and/or that the querent (the person consulting the tarot) is beginning a new cycle in his or her growth. A spread with many high-numbered cards indicates that the matter is nearing completion and/or that the querent has reached a level of maturity with regard to the subject of the reading. (Spreads and readings are discussed in chapter 3.)

Tarot Symbolism

Occult knowledge has often been feared by the "powers that be." (*Occult*, by the way, means hidden.) Therefore, the tarot's early practitioners passed along this body of wisdom through symbols and imagery to avoid persecution and to protect the information from being destroyed. The symbolism on the cards draws on numerous occult traditions and systems, including the Cabala, numerology, astrology, alchemy, and various schools of magical thought.

In addition to the main symbolism of the suits, you'll notice several images appearing regularly on tarot cards. We also find these symbols in other contexts, including art, literature, religion, occult practices, dreams, psychology, advertising, and politics. As I wrote in my book *Magickal Astrology*, "Symbols speak to us at an unconscious level, evoking truths, archetypes, emotions, and spiritual qualities that lie at the core of our psyches." They embody the essence of the things they stand for and encompass universal concepts, transcending the boundaries of culture, geography, and time.

Geometric shapes are frequently depicted on tarot cards to express specific qualities or ideas. Circles represent wholeness and unity. Squares connote stability. Spirals depict life energy. Upward-pointing triangles signify the archetypal male force; downward-pointing triangles stand for the archetypal female force. Crosses, six-pointed stars, and Egyptian ankhs show the integration of male and female, body and spirit, heaven and earth.

Celestial images are popular symbols, too. The sun represents clarity, vision, vitality, happiness, masculine energy. The moon is associated with intuition, emotion, cycles of growth or decline, secrets, feminine energy. Stars denote hope, awareness, and spirit made manifest in the physical world; they may also be configured as actual zodiac constellations. Astrological glyphs often appear on tarot cards, too, because these two esoteric arts are integrally entwined.

Crowns, scepters, and thrones are obvious symbols of power and dominion. Snakes signify wisdom, occult power, kundalini energy, sexuality, and transformation. Roses denote love, both human and divine. Arrows stand for will, inspiration, spirit, and focused thought. Birds and animals represent the qualities found in their real-life counterparts. Trees indicate growth, strength, time, and ancient wisdom. Mountains suggest a quest or a challenge that must be faced and surmounted. Other symbols may be drawn from specific cultures or schools of thought—especially in decks that emphasize a particular tradition, ethnic background, or spiritual path—and some may have personal significance for the deck's creator. In the tarot deck I'm designing, for instance, I incorporate Celtic knotwork and labyrinths to represent life's twists and turns.

The tarot uses color symbolically, too. Colors mean different things in different cultures, however—white, for instance, represents purity in Western society, but it's the color of mourning in China. Many tarot decks link colors with the four elements—yellow = air, blue = water, green = earth, and red = fire. Some artists draw on the psychological implications of color to illustrate ideas.

In this sense, pink stands for love, red for passion and assertiveness, orange for action and warmth, blue for serenity, green for growth and health, yellow for optimism, purple for wisdom and power, black for mystery, brown for stability and grounding.

Symbols not only provide decorative touches on tarot cards, they enable information to be quickly conveyed through the language of imagery. Even if you don't consciously understand the meanings of these symbols, your inner knowing will recognize and respond to them.

Chapter 3

Tarot Readings

The tarot can be used in many ways—to gain insight into a problem or situation, to divine the future, as an aid to meditation, or in magical work. In my book *10-Minute Magic Spells*, I include a number of spells that utilize tarot cards. In *10-Minute Crystal Ball*, I offer tips for using them to enhance intuition.

In what's known as a *reading*, cards are drawn individually from a deck or laid out in special arrangements or patterns called *spreads*. A reading can be as simple as selecting one card from the deck to provide food for thought during the day. Complex readings involving several different spreads may be done to examine a concern from a variety of angles, provide insight into more than one related issue, or give an overview of your life.

Readings cover only a relatively short span of time, usually no more than a few months. It isn't very productive to inquire about something in the distant future. If a thirteen-year-old girl asks what sort of man she'll marry, for instance, the tarot will respond—based on conditions at the moment—but the reply probably won't be very useful. That's because your attitudes and behavior, as well as circumstances outside your control, will affect matters between now and then, thereby altering your future. In my opinion, the future isn't fixed—it is fluid and influenced by every thought, feeling, and action. Interestingly, I've found that if I change my outlook or behavior, the cards will offer different advice or indicate a different outcome after only a day or so.

A tarot reading is not a parlor game—don't approach it with skepticism or amusement, or test the oracle to see if it will correctly respond to a question whose answer you already know. Think of a reading as a private audience with an all-knowing stage. Respect the oracle and the source from which the information comes. Regardless of the type of reading you do, be sincere and trust that the tarot will offer helpful advice.

The more important the matter is to you and the clearer your request, the more likely you are to get good advice. "Garbage in, garbage out" certainly applies in tarot readings.

Here are some tips.
- Don't ask several questions at once.
- Ask about what's foremost in your mind first, then, if you wish, move on to other topics. Often the tarot will respond to your most pressing concern, even if you ask about something else.

- If you don't like the answer, don't ask the same question again, hoping you'll get a response you prefer.
- If you don't understand the answer, ask for further illumination or ask a different, but related question.
- Don't ask ambiguous questions. Early one December, I did a reading for a woman whose husband had terminal cancer. She asked if he would be with her at Christmas. The tarot answered "yes." When he died mid-month, she thought the cards had been mistaken. But on Christmas Day the woman felt her husband's presence so strongly that she knew he was, indeed, with her.
- Don't do a reading when you're tired or distracted.
- Alcohol and other mood-altering substances can affect a reading and produce an unclear or inaccurate response.

Laying Out the Cards

Often a reading begins with either the reader or the querent choosing a *significator*, a card that represents the person for whom the reading is being done. Some people intentionally select a card that corresponds to their astrological sign, age, profession, or other characteristics. A forty-six-year-old banker might relate to the king of pentacles, for instance. Others prefer to draw a card randomly from the deck to stand as the significator.

Although the significator is often a "person" card (court card, The High Priestess, The Emperor, etc.), it doesn't have to be. Usually, a randomly chosen card will quite accurately depict your state of being or your primary interest at the time of the reading. If you're about to go on a trip, you might intuitively select a knight; if you are concerned about a legal matter, you might choose Justice as your significator. This card reveals something about you and, at the same time, connects you in a very personal way with the reading.

Before you begin laying out the cards, take a few minutes to calm and center yourself. Contemplate your question or concern while you shuffle the cards. Blow on them if you wish. When you feel ready, cut the cards with your "other" hand (the one you don't normally write with), then lay out your spread from the top of the second pile with the cards face up. If you prefer, you can shuffle the cards and then fan them out in front of you, face down. Choose one or more cards from the fan and arrange them in a spread.

Several of my favorite spreads are discussed below. I suggest you try them all, then continue using the ones that suit your purposes. If you like, you can modify these or design your own original spreads.

✦ Single-Card Method

The simplest of all readings, this can be done every morning to give you food for thought during the day or to provide guidance about a particular matter, especially an ongoing one such as a relationship or job.

Follow the steps above, cut the deck, and turn over the top card. That's your answer or advice for the day. You may want to use this card in meditation or display it someplace where you'll see it often throughout the day.

✦ Past–Present–Future Spread

Shuffle and cut the cards, and draw from the top of the second pile. Lay out three cards, face up, from left to right. The card on the left represents the past or the foundation of the matter, the middle card describes the situation at present, and the right-hand card reveals the future.

✦ Four-Card Spread

Shuffle and cut the cards. Lay out four cards, face up, from left to right. The card on the left represents the situation at present, the second card shows the obstacle or challenge before you, the third suggests the action you should take, and the right-hand card reveals the outcome.

✦ This or That Spread

Use this simple method when you're trying to decide between two options. Shuffle and cut the cards. Turn over one card to show what you can expect if you choose option A. Turn over a second card to indicate what's likely to happen if you go with option B.

✦ Yes–No Spread

This method answers yes-or-no questions. Shuffle and cut the cards. Start turning cards over, one by one, into a pile until you come to an ace or have counted out thirteen cards. Stop and begin a second pile, laying out the cards in the same manner. Stop when you turn up an ace or have laid out thirteen cards. Make a third pile the same way.

If the result is three upright aces, the answer is a definite yes. If you got three upside-down aces, the answer is a definite no. Two upright aces means yes, but what you do may still have an effect on the outcome. Two reversed aces indicates no, but there still may be some room for change. One upright ace and one upside-down ace suggests uncertainty—the situation is still in flux or could go either way. If only one ace or none appears, an answer cannot be determined at present.

Often, the suits of the aces will describe the nature of your concern. The top card on a pile of thirteen may show conditions surrounding the question or suggest actions you could take.

I once did a reading for a woman who was recovering from cancer surgery. She asked if the cancer was gone. The tarot responded with two upright aces and one pile of thirteen cards with the queen of pentacles on top. I interpreted the answer as yes, but that she needed to take care of herself physically to keep the cancer from returning.

✦ Karma–Dharma Spread

This spread provides insight into a particular area of your life by showing what possibilities exist for you and what's keeping you from actualizing them. Shuffle and cut the cards.

Lay the first card, face up, on the table. This card describes the present situation or the subject of the reading. Turn up a second card and position it above the first. This card signifies your *dharma*—your goals, calling, potential, or options in life, what you should be reaching for or striving to achieve. Place a third card, face up, beneath the first card. This card shows your *karma,* the self-limiting attitudes, actions, and so on in your past (either your childhood or previous lifetimes) that are blocking or undermining your success.

✦ Simple Cross

This pattern combines the Past–Present–Future Spread with the Karma–Dharma Spread. Shuffle and cut the cards, then lay them out in this order:

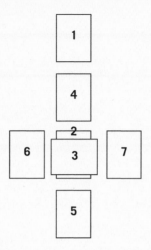

Card #1 = significator

Card #2 = the present situation or subject of the reading

Card #3 = the obstacle or opportunity influencing the present situation

Card #4 = hopes and dreams, your possibilities, goals, potential,
what you want most and should be striving to achieve

Card #5 = what's beneath you, weaknesses, old baggage, attitudes,
or behaviors that may be holding you back

Card #6 = recent past

Card #7 = near future

✦ Celtic Cross Spread

The most popular tarot spread, the Celtic Cross can be used to gain insight into just about any situation or concern. Notice that it expands upon the previous spread. Shuffle and cut the cards, then lay them out in this order:

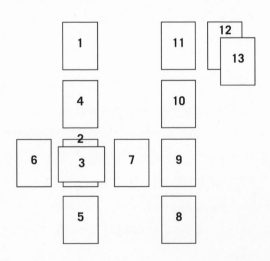

Card #1 = significator

Card #2 = the present situation or subject of the reading

Card #3 = the obstacle or opportunity influencing the present situation

Card #4 = hopes and dreams, your possibilities, goals, potential, what you want most and should be striving to achieve

Card #5 = difficulties in the past, weaknesses, what's beneath you, things that may be holding you back

Card #6 = the last of the present, the recent past, what's just happened or is about to move out of your life

Card #7 = the first of the future, what will transpire in the near future, usually within the next few days or so

Card #8 = the future environment, the conditions you'll experience in the coming days, weeks, or months with respect to the subject of the reading

Card #9 = people around you, friends, coworkers, loved ones, enemies, etc., who will play a part in the situation as it unfolds

Card #10 = the turning point, what you could do to produce or
influence the outcome; some people say this position
shows your hopes as well as your fears about the subject
of the reading

Card #11 = the outcome, what's most likely to occur

Cards #12 and #13 = further amplification of the outcome (if necessary)
to explain in greater detail or expand on the subject of the
reading; generally these cards are used only when the
outcome card is an ace or a trump

✦ Horoscope Spread

This is a good spread to do on your birthday to see what's in store for you in the coming months. It can also provide information and advice about how to constructively handle the various parts of your life. Each house in a horoscope or astrological chart deals with specific areas of life. Shuffle and cut the cards, then place one face up in each of the twelve houses, forming a circle.

Interpret the cards in relation to the areas associated with each house. If The Sun falls as Card #10, for instance, it indicates that you are clear about your professional goals and the public views you as a strong, confident, creative leader. The three of pentacles in position #6 could show that productively applying your skills will help you to successfully complete a phase of your work. This spread can either show specific outcomes or events in the areas of life that correspond to particular houses or offer advice about how to utilize related energies and abilities.

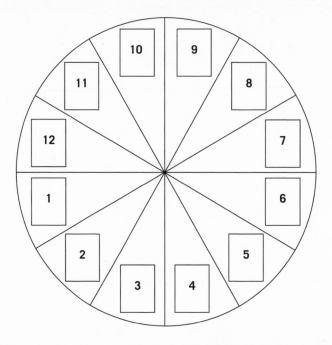

Card #1 = significator, your physical appearance, how you want to
           be seen, the first impression you give others

Card #2 = finances, resources, values, abilities you can use to earn money

Card #3 = siblings, neighbors, early education, mundane or
           practical information, short trips

Card #4 = home, childhood, parents, security, your roots

Card #5 = creativity, self-expression, children, love affairs, recreation, things to which you devote love

Card #6 = work, coworkers, duties, service, health (especially as it relates to work)

Card #7 = partnerships in love or business, agents, consultants

Card #8 = partner's resources, other people's money, inheritance, death/transformation, occult knowledge, hidden power

Card #9 = higher knowledge, advanced education, religion, philosophy, long-distance travel, publishing

Card #10 = public image, reputation, career, business relationships, how the world sees you

Card #11 = friends, group activities, professional organizations, goals and objectives, things from which you derive validation and encouragement

Card #12 = hidden resources, undeveloped parts of yourself, secret enemies, your shadow side, things that undermine you

✦ Feng Shui Spread

This pattern utilizes the bagua, an eight-sided map feng shui practitioners use to analyze your home. In feng shui theory, each section of your home relates to a particular area of life. Shuffle and cut the cards, then place one face up in each of the nine sectors, or gua.

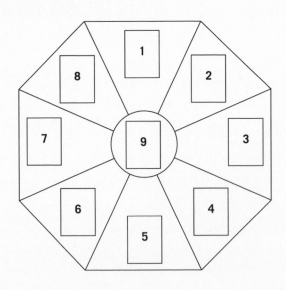

Interpret the cards in relation to the areas associated with each gua. For example, if The Star turned up as Card #1, you should remain hopeful about your future, for success and recognition are likely. The seven of swords as Card #6 could indicate that you have a unique spiritual or intellectual perspective and should follow your own path. (To learn more about feng shui, see my book *10-Minute Feng Shui*.)

Card #1 = fame, public image, future

Card #2 = relationships, marriage, love

Card #3 = creativity, children, self-expression

Card #4 = helpful people, friends, colleagues, travel

Card #5 = self, identity, work, purpose in life

Card #6 = knowledge, spirituality

Card #7 = community, family, neighbors

Card #8 = wealth, prosperity

Card #9 = health and well-being

✦ Relationship Spread

This triangular-shaped spread can be used to provide insight into any type of relationship involving two people—love, business, family, friendship, even one between enemies. Shuffle and cut the cards, then lay them out, face up, in this order:

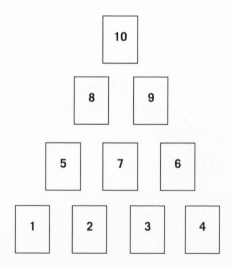

Card #1 = the past, the foundation of the relationship, the karmic connection between those in the relationship

Card #2 = the present situation or concern

Card #3 = the obstacle or opportunity presented by this relationship

Card #4 = how you should handle this obstacle or opportunity

Card #5 = your role, what you bring to the relationship

Card #6 = the other person's role, what he or she brings to the relationship

Card #7 = the entity you form together

Card #8 = what you truly want or expect from the relationship

Card #9 = what the other person truly wants or expects from the relationship

Card #10 = the outcome

Interpreting the Cards

The tarot speaks directly to your subconscious or intuition by using the language of symbols. Before you begin analyzing a spread, take a few moments to gaze at the cards without intellectualizing about them. Let the entire pattern impress itself on you. Notice any feelings and insights that arise.

Start with a broad overview and work down to specifics. Look at the colors and images on the cards. What do they say to you?

Does one suit predominate? Is any suit absent? The suits describe basic energies or modes of functioning, as well as the subject of the reading and the factors influencing the situation.

Do lots of court cards appear in the spread? This suggests the presence of many people around you or that others play key roles in the matter.

Are more than half the cards in the spread from the major arcana? Major arcana cards indicate that fate or forces outside your control are operating and guiding the situation. Spiritual or inner growth may be more important than physical results.

Consider the numbers on the cards. Do any numbers predominate? These can show cycles or the degree to which a situation has developed.

Look for connections between the cards. Do certain types of cards turn up in "past" positions, for instance? Is growth or progress indicated from "past" cards to "future" cards? For example, a princess occupying a past position in a spread and a queen in a future position shows development over the time period covered by the reading.

Finally, examine the meaning of each individual card, taking its position in the spread, its relationship to the other cards, and all other factors into account. Until you are adept at interpreting the cards, use the information in

Part Two of this book to help you. I also recommend reading other books on the tarot, for each author will give you a slightly different take on the cards, based on his or her own perspective, philosophy, and experiences.

Let your intuition guide you. If you feel that a card means something different to you than to the "experts," go with your own impressions. In a sense, tarot readings are like dreams—they are highly personal and should be seen as a way to communicate with your own inner knowing.

It's a good idea to keep a journal of your readings. Doing so will help you learn from them and improve your interpretive ability. You'll also be able to chart your personal development over time.

Reversed Cards

As you shuffle and handle the cards, some of them may get turned upside down. When you lay them out in a spread, they appear "reversed." Tarot books present various ideas about and explanations of reversed cards.

Generally speaking, a reversed card indicates a blockage, imbalance, or improper utilization of the energy symbolized by the card. For instance, the six of swords in an upright position suggests improvement, escaping difficulties, and moving to a better stage. Reversed, this card could mean running away from problems rather than addressing them. Some tarot researchers suggest that reversed cards describe the "shadow side" of the energies, what lies behind the outer expression, or things you don't want to acknowledge and deal with. Others say that a reversed card's meaning is the opposite of its upright meaning.

In the beginning, until you become more familiar with the tarot, you may want to consider only upright cards. If you draw a reversed card, simply reposition it and read it upright. In time, you can explore reversed cards and come to your own understanding of their meanings.

How Often Should You Do Readings?

How often should you do readings? That depends on your reason for wanting to know something, what's going on in your life, what kind of information you seek, what type of reading you do, and many other factors. I recommend doing a general reading at least four times a year, on the equinoxes and solstices. Your birthday is also a good date for a reading. The Horoscope Spread discussed earlier in this chapter can provide insight into the coming year.

I do a Celtic Cross Spread for myself each month to provide an overview. I also do one on each of the eight Pagan holidays. If I need advice about a particular matter, I'll use the Celtic Cross or another spread that's appropriate to the question. Sometimes I'll lay out more than one spread, approaching the question from different perspectives. I also draw one card each morning to contemplate its meaning and guide me through the day.

Occasionally, the cards get tired. Perhaps you've over-worked them or asked about the same issue so often that there's nothing more to tell at this time. When this happens, you may find that the cards you select don't seem to relate to the matter at hand. I often draw the four of swords or the ten of swords when it's time to take a break. Set the cards aside for a few days and let them rest. You may want to give yourself a rest, too. If you decide to continue doing readings during this period, use another deck—or a different oracle.

Part Two, Chapter 4

Pentacles

The suit of pentacles, sometimes called *coins* or *discs*, represents the element of earth. These cards describe situations involving money, work, and property, as well as physical conditions and practical concerns. In an ordinary playing deck, diamonds are the equivalent of pentacles.

Ace of Pentacles

✦ In questions about money

The ace points to a new business venture, investment, or other financial project. A moneymaking opportunity may soon come your way. This is the time to sow seeds. Tend a new endeavor carefully and it will bear fruit.

✦ In questions about love

You could meet a romantic partner who offers you financial security or material comfort. Perhaps you'll encounter this person through your work. In some cases, the ace shows that you have or should take a practical, down-to-earth attitude toward a new partnership. It may also represent the early stages of a relationship based mainly on physical attraction.

✦ In questions about work

The ace indicates the start of a new job, project, or business. Or, you could receive financial backing for a venture. During this early stage, you should be prepared to work hard to get the budding endeavor off the ground.

✦ As a card for personal growth

You are beginning to address practical matters—or should. The ace can also advise you to pay attention to your health. Meditate on this card to become more grounded or pragmatic.

Two of Pentacles

✦ **In questions about money**

The two of pentacles symbolizes the early development of a financial or physical endeavor. Don't initiate major changes or expect big results at this time. Money may come in and go out quickly, finances might be unstable, and you may have to juggle your resources. It can also indicate two sources of income.

✦ **In questions about love**

You may feel impatient or restless in a relationship. Some adjustments might be necessary at this time, as you reassess what you want. Perhaps you and/or your partner need to handle responsibilities or money matters in a more balanced way. This card can also represent shared resources.

✦ In questions about work

Changes in your job or work environment are likely, resulting in instability and uncertainty. Perhaps you feel impatient because you don't see much progress being made. Budget your time, energy, and resources. Be content with small changes and slow growth. This card can also represent two jobs or two ways of earning money.

✦ As a card for personal growth

The two signifies a period of restlessness and uncertainty with regard to practical or physical matters. Work on developing your skills and resources slowly—it may take a while before you notice much progress. Pay attention to the process as well as the goal.

Three of Pentacles

✦ **In questions about money**

You can earn money through the practical investment of your energy, talents, or resources. This card may signal the successful completion of a stage in a financial venture. It can also recommend honing your skills in order to increase your income.

✦ **In questions about love**

The three can indicate a "payback" period, when you receive dividends on the investment you've made in a relationship and see the results of your efforts materialize. After working to overcome challenges, you find contentment and can finally enjoy each other.

✦ In questions about work

The three represents the constructive utilization of your abilities to produce lasting, physical results. Explore ways to earn money from your effort and talents, or seek a job that enables you to actualize your abilities. Sometimes this card means that you will successfully complete a project or end a job on good terms.

✦ As a card for personal growth

The card of the artisan who combines creativity with practicality, the three describes the process of applying your ideas and talents in useful ways. It can also signify the completion of a stage in your personal development. Meditating on this card can help you bring your dreams to fruition.

Four of Pentacles

✦ **In questions about money**

The four represents a solidification and concentration of money and/or resources. You are accumulating wealth or have sound financial backing. In some cases, this card tells you an investment is solid. It can also suggest that you are too concerned with acquiring money and security.

✦ **In questions about love**

This card describes a stable, committed partnership. However, it can also suggest a relationship that has become too structured and lacks freedom or excitement. In some instances, the four symbolizes a relationship based mainly on money and security.

✦   **In questions about work**

A work situation is stable and financially secure. Your abilities are valued and enable you to earn a good income. However, you may remain in a job you no longer enjoy because it provides security. This card also symbolizes the power and status that come with money.

✦   **As a card for personal growth**

Apply your ideas and creativity in ways that produce stability. Perhaps you need to strengthen your self-worth and find security within yourself. Meditate on this card to improve your self-esteem.

Five of Pentacles

✦ **In questions about money**

Sometimes associated with poverty and scarcity, the five of pentacles also represents freedom from the responsibilities that come with having money and property. It can mean that you emphasize spiritual issues rather than financial ones. Simplify your lifestyle, paring down your possessions to the necessities. An investment made now might not pay off.

✦ **In questions about love**

It's time to free yourself from people who drain your resources—emotional, creative, or physical. You no longer choose to be responsible for someone else, preferring the simplicity of a solo existence.

✦ In questions about work

The five of pentacles can indicate that you aren't earning enough in your job or feel strained by work-related responsibilities. Perhaps you aren't using your talents in your work or don't receive the rewards you deserve. It may be time to seek a more satisfying occupation.

✦ As a card for personal growth

The five symbolizes wasted effort, talent, or resources. Work on developing your self-worth from the inside out, instead of equating "worth" with money and possessions. What you sacrifice financially now will pay off in spiritual terms.

Six of Pentacles

✦ **In questions about money**

The six of pentacles symbolizes shared resources and prosperity. You might have an opportunity to participate in a financial venture or partnership that promises mutual benefits. By allying yourself with another person or group, you may be able to earn greater profits. This card can also mean that you will receive financial backing.

✦ **In questions about love**

Give-and-take is important now. Share your resources—financial and otherwise—with a partner so that both of you can prosper. Be receptive to what the other person offers. The six of pentacles can also represent a business or moneymaking venture with a romantic partner.

✦ In questions about work

The six symbolizes teamwork, group ventures, and business partnerships. You have a better chance of success if you share resources and responsibilities with people whose abilities and assets complement yours. You may have an opportunity to join others in a worthwhile project or business.

✦ As a card for personal growth

Learn the value of give-and-take. Allow others to help you and be willing to assist them in return. If you become more generous with your energy, talents, and other resources, you'll discover that people reciprocate in kind.

Seven of Pentacles

✦ **In questions about money**

The harvest is still a long way off. You can't rush things, so be patient and persevering. Don't give up hope during this period of slow, steady development. Avoid "get rich quick" schemes and anything that seems too good to be true.

✦ **In questions about love**

You may feel you aren't making much progress or that a relationship isn't turning out as you'd hoped, but this card advises you to be patient. Keep working at it, taking small steps toward your goal. You still have a long way to go before you reach the end of this matter.

✦ In questions about work

Patience and persistence are needed now. Pay attention to details and do your best at all you undertake. Continue applying your energy and resources toward your goal. The effort you put in now will pay off at a later date.

✦ As a card for personal growth

You've already put forth a lot of effort, but the end still isn't in sight. Don't get discouraged. Instead, keep developing your self-worth and your abilities at your own pace. Meditate on this card to help you become more patient.

Eight of Pentacles

✦ In questions about money

You may have to spend money to make money. This card advises you to give it your all and go to whatever lengths are necessary to achieve your financial goals. A financial venture could require effort and focus. In some cases, the eight indicates that you may need more expertise before you can profit.

✦ In questions about love

Dedicate yourself to making your relationship work. If you want more love in your life, you have to be more loving. View this as an opportunity for learning and growth. Like any other endeavor, a relationship requires work and will benefit from sincere effort. Sometimes the eight represents a romance that comes late in life.

✦ In questions about work

Apply yourself diligently and perfect your abilities. For a time, you may have to completely immerse yourself in your work. Perhaps you need to acquire more skill or knowledge in a particular area. Set realistic goals and work hard to become the best you can possibly be.

✦ As a card for personal growth

Continue striving for excellence. Keep your eyes on your goal and work hard to achieve it. Learn as much as you can and don't take shortcuts. Sometimes this card advises you to get serious about improving your health.

Nine of Pentacles

✦ In questions about money

The nine of pentacles represents financial success and physical comfort. You can now enjoy a period of accomplishment, when you will be adequately rewarded for your efforts. You make good use of your resources and reap benefits accordingly. An investment entered into at this time should pay off.

✦ In questions about love

This card depicts fulfillment and security in a relationship. You have weathered storms and persevered through good times and bad; now you can enjoy the pleasures you've earned. The nine can also symbolize a relationship that provides financial abundance and/or physical satisfaction.

✦ In questions about work

The nine promises success, recognition, and rewards for your work. You take charge of your career path and can reach a position of leadership, for others respect your abilities and accomplishments. Through your own efforts and talent, you achieve much. Enjoy this time of fulfillment— you've earned it.

✦ As a card for personal growth

Your sense of self-worth is strong and you are in full command of your abilities and resources. Now you can use your knowledge, money, and/or skills to help others.

Ten of Pentacles

✦ In questions about money

The ten of pentacles represents wealth and/or property. You may receive an inheritance, or family money might be available to use for your own purposes. Prosperity and abundance are likely. This card can also indicate investments in large-scale projects or philanthropic ventures.

✦ In questions about love

The ten indicates happiness, security, and fulfillment. A relationship may support the development of your talents or strengthen your sense of self-worth. Home and family are key words for this card, so it can mean you are ready to establish your own family. In some instances, the ten shows marriage into a family with money and/or status.

✦ In questions about work

This card shows success in the outer world. Fame and fortune can be yours, for you possess the necessary abilities to accomplish much. Use your skills and resources to help others by taking part in humanitarian projects or working for the greater good.

✦ As a card for personal growth

The ten symbolizes inner strength, security, and a strong sense of your own worth. This may come from a supportive family situation or through your own efforts and achievements. Your personal power can inspire other people. Meditate on this card to increase your self-worth and inner security.

Princess (or Page) of Pentacles

✦ **In questions about money**

The princess of pentacles represents contracts, paperwork, or negotiations concerning money. Carefully analyze investments and financial documents—pay attention to details. Learn all you can about money matters. Be practical and don't allow emotions to influence financial decisions.

✦ **In questions about love**

This card shows a down-to-earth, uncomplicated approach to relationships. Sincerity is important. A partnership described by the princess of pentacles emphasizes practical matters and mundane concerns and probably isn't very romantic or exciting.

✦ **In questions about work**

The princess represents work in a practical field or in a support position, perhaps in a health-related area or the trades. It can also indicate training or an entry-level position. Your job provides financial security, but not much glamour or excitement. Money and stability may be more important than self-expression or fame.

✦ As someone you know

The princess represents a practical, no-nonsense person (male or female). Although young, he or she is responsible, hardworking, and capable and can be depended on in both personal and professional matters. This card describes someone who is unemotional and detached, a loner who is content to lead a simple life. Sometimes it shows a person who loves nature.

✦ As a card for personal growth

Tend to practical matters and the everyday details of life. You may be called upon to fulfill a duty or perform a service to others. This card might also advise you to take care of your health.

Prince (or Knight) of Pentacles

✦ **In questions about money**

Money comes to you as a result of honest labor or secure investments. In some cases, this card symbolizes land or other property. Be practical with money and stabilize your financial situation—don't take risks. Expect slow, steady gains rather than windfalls.

✦ **In questions about love**

This card indicates stability and loyalty in a relationship. A partnership may be based on practical considerations, financial security, and/or physical pleasure. In some cases, the prince recommends patience, fidelity, and being more realistic about your partner and yourself.

✦ In questions about work

Self-reliance is called for now. You must succeed on your own through hard work, perseverance, and dependability. This card can also symbolize a job producing something useful, such as farming, manufacturing, or construction.

✦ As someone you know

The prince represents a straightforward, honest, dependable individual (male or female) who is interested in nature and/or the physical side of life. Though not unintelligent, he or she may lack sophistication, experience, or education. This person deftly handles practical tasks and enjoys simple pleasures.

✦ As a card for personal growth

Take care of mundane, physical, or financial matters. Be honest, patient, practical, gentle, and dependable in all areas of life. Personal growth may come through helping others.

Queen of Pentacles

✦ In questions about money

Financial gain comes through business ventures or sound investments. Use money and other resources in constructive, creative ways and you'll prosper. Manage your money wisely. Joint financial ventures could also prove advantageous.

✦ In questions about love

The queen of pentacles describes a mature relationship between people who are sincere in their affection. An alliance is based on common goals and respect. Contentment, creature comforts, sensual pleasure, security, and mutual support are possible in this partnership.

✦ In questions about work

The queen represents partnership, teamwork, and joint projects. You have a good head for business and a knack for managing people. A job promises financial rewards. Other people may depend on you for financial support or your job might involve helping others, perhaps in a health-related field.

✦ **As someone you know**

The queen symbolizes a mature, capable woman, often someone who is good at business or successful in her chosen vocation. Usually she is fond of sensual pleasures—good food, sex, nice clothes, and creature comforts—and might even be a bit indulgent. Independent and self-confident, she knows what she wants and how to get it.

✦ **As a card for personal growth**

The queen stands for mastery in the physical world. This card advises you to gain control over material and financial matters. Accept, care for, and enjoy your own body. Meditate on the queen to help you bring your dreams to fruition.

King of Pentacles

✦ In questions about money

Financial security and monetary success can be yours, but you must take responsibility for how you use and invest resources. Your chances of attaining prosperity and abundance are good. Sometimes this card shows you controlling the flow of money or handling investments wisely, perhaps on a large scale. Good organization and sound money management are necessary now.

✦ In questions about love

This card signifies a serious and mature partnership between people who support each other's growth and well-being. However, the relationship might be based mainly on financial considerations, status, or security. A partnership may be stable and comfortable, but not very stimulating or romantic.

✦ In questions about work

The king represents the business world and indicates success in a business venture, a stable career, or through managing material resources. Good organization, courage, honesty, and determination will help you to achieve your goals. Put your energies toward developing something that will endure.

✦ As someone you know

The king symbolizes a mature, responsible man who is a respected leader. Often he can be found in the business world or financial sector. Practical, hardworking, and courageous, he is a good provider and a loyal friend. However, he can be too rigid and unemotional, preferring work to personal relationships.

✦ As a card for personal growth

Organization and practicality are needed. Develop your resources and become more self-sufficient. Meditate on this card to hone your courage, leadership ability, and common sense so you can tackle problems with confidence.

Chapter 5

Swords

The suit of swords describes situations involving communication, intellectual pursuits, reason, ideas, and analysis. These cards represent the element of air. In an ordinary playing deck, spades are interpreted as swords.

Ace of Swords

✦ **In questions about money**

The ace marks the birth of a new idea that could be profitable. It may also represent an investment or business venture involving communication. Concentrate on your objective and trust your own judgment. In some cases, this card signifies the first stages of negotiating a contract or legal matter involving money.

✦ **In questions about love**

A relationship based on shared ideas and friendship may begin soon. The ace can also symbolize a partner who is mentally oriented and emotionally detached. Sometimes this card indicates a need to open the channels of communication or discuss relationship issues in an objective, forthright manner.

✦ In questions about work

The ace represents the start of a project or occupation that utilizes your intellect, communication skills, and/or information channels. Concentrate totally on your goal— don't let anything distract you or dissipate your energy. In some cases, you may need to further your education in order to improve your job prospects.

✦ As a card for personal growth

The ace of swords symbolizes mental clarity and focus. Perhaps you need to be more objective and rational. This card can also herald an important new idea or perspective.

Two of Swords

✦ **In questions about money**

A difference of opinion exists regarding an investment or moneymaking venture. In times of uncertainty, don't allow other people to confuse you—have faith in your own ideas. Cover your bases and watch out for loopholes in contracts, investments, and other financial documents.

✦ **In questions about love**

A delicate situation seems peaceful, but discord may continue to simmer beneath the surface. Some matters still need to be resolved. Good communication and compromise are required to overcome obstacles in a relationship. This card can also suggest that two people have very different perspectives.

✦ In questions about work

Lack of clarity causes confusion in a work-related matter. Have faith in yourself and take care of details, even though you may not be sure of the outcome. Sometimes the two of swords shows a stalemate due to a difference of opinion. A tricky situation might require tact and perspicacity. Don't push it—at a later date you can address the problem directly.

✦ As a card for personal growth

You can't see the forest for the trees. Because the future is unclear, you must rely on blind faith. This card may also indicate that you need to develop focus, be more rational, or learn more about a subject. Seek peace and balance.

Three of Swords

✦ In questions about money

Losses or suffering result from relying totally on analysis and rational thinking while ignoring your intuition. The three of swords may also represent money made at the expense of other values, or in a way that hurts you or others.

✦ In questions about love

A chasm exists between you and the person you love. Quarrels and discord may divide you, or circumstances may cause a physical separation. Pain and suffering result. Try to bridge the gap with understanding, compassion, and honest communication.

✦ In questions about work

You aren't doing the work you love and feel isolated, unhappy, or remorseful as a result. From this discontent comes awareness. Once you decide what you really want, you can seek a more fulfilling vocation. Creative people may be able to use this melancholic period to produce inspired work.

✦ As a card for personal growth

The three describes an imbalance between head and heart. The mind has dominated, causing feelings of alienation and sadness. Take steps to reunite with whatever nourishes your soul.

Four of Swords

✦ In questions about money

Discrimination is needed. Consider a financial matter carefully, without seeking input from others. Perhaps you should withdraw from a situation and wait for a better time to act. In some cases, the four advises you to detach yourself from money and possessions, especially if you feel overburdened by financial responsibilities.

✦ In questions about love

You need to withdraw and pull yourself together. Stress, upsets, or quarrels with a partner may have exhausted you; now you need to rest. Through enforced solitude, you can gain clarity and objectivity.

✦ In questions about work

You feel burned out and dispirited. You need to take some time off to get your head together and renew your strength after a period of confusion and stress. Take a vacation, if possible. Don't let other people drain you. Withdraw physically or emotionally until you regain your balance.

✦ As a card for personal growth

The four of swords represents solitude and contemplation. Instead of trying to deal with challenges in the outer world, tend to your inner world through meditation, rest, and spiritual practice.

Five of Swords

✦ In questions about money

Indecision and confusion may be causing difficulties in a financial matter. The five of swords can also represent arguments or differences of opinion regarding money. Other people's input may be interfering with your ability to act or see things clearly. Stop vacillating and be firm. Sometimes this card suggests that you are out of your league. Accept limitations or setbacks with dignity.

✦ In questions about love

You may be trying to move or make changes too quickly. Discord and confusion result. Although it's important to listen to your own heart and mind, remain open to possibilities and try to see the other person's side of things, too. Strive for understanding rather than merely attempting to get your own way.

✦ In questions about work

Before you can progress, you need to listen and learn more. Confusion keeps you from acting or making decisions. Perhaps vacillation has resulted in setbacks or lost opportunities. Recognize your limitations, seek clarity, and avoid challenges from other people. Don't make enemies now.

✦ As a card for personal growth

You need to develop clarity so you can follow your own truth. Rather than trying to gain ground at this time, accept your limitations and learn more before trying to advance.

Six of Swords

✦ **In questions about money**

You have the information you need to make informed decisions about financial matters. Past difficulties can be resolved now. Travel may play a role in making money. In some cases, this card advises you to give up a financial venture and move on to something more lucrative.

✦ **In questions about love**

The six represents a time of harmony and happiness. You and a partner can communicate easily and agree on important issues. Now is the time to put problems behind you. Think positive—it has a beneficial effect on all your relationships. Sometimes this card shows you leaving an unhappy partnership for a more satisfying one.

✦ In questions about work

After a stressful period, things improve. Your goal is within reach and can be achieved by applying the knowledge you've gained. Use your connections to help you advance. Perhaps you'll be taking a business trip soon. Sometimes the six of swords advises you to leave an unfulfilling job and go on to a better one that offers you more freedom, intellectual rapport, or opportunity.

✦ As a card for personal growth

The six of swords symbolizes mental clarity and understanding. The knowledge you possess can take you far. This is also a good time to study or embark on a journey (physical or spiritual). All your experiences propel you toward the ultimate goal of enlightenment. Meditate on this card to help you find the answers to questions.

Seven of Swords

✦ In questions about money

Think for yourself in financial areas. You can profit from using your own information, experience, or connections. If a situation is too limiting or doesn't meet your criteria, you may want to look elsewhere. Negative attitudes may be interfering with your prosperity. This card can also represent a breakthrough.

✦ In questions about love

Stand up for what you think is right and don't let someone else call all the shots—but be diplomatic rather than quarrelsome with a partner. Think positive. Compromise is the best solution. If that isn't possible, you may decide to seek a relationship with someone who shares your ideas or one that allows you more intellectual freedom.

✦ In questions about work

You need intellectual freedom and diversity. If your current job doesn't allow this, perhaps you should consider moving on. Some plans may need to be revised. Avoid direct confrontation and arguments.

✦ As a card for personal growth

Keep an open mind. Respect other people's ideas as well as your own. Exploring new ideas or unconventional philosophies could benefit you. Examine how your thoughts influence your life.

Eight of Swords

✦ **In questions about money**

Your progress may be hampered by obstacles or interference from others. Inconsistency or wasted energy could result in losses. Don't undermine yourself or get into a position where your hands are tied. Consolidate your resources instead of diversifying. Small gains are possible, but don't expect megabucks.

✦ **In questions about love**

The problems you are experiencing are of your own making. Fear, lack of persistence, and/or misunderstanding prevent you from being happy. Accept limitations, but don't close yourself off to possibilities. Be clear about what's really important. Sometimes improving your attitude can improve your relationship.

✦ In questions about work

You may be wasting effort or misusing your talent/ideas. Rather than scattering your energy, focus on one thing and be persistent. Don't let your fears hold you back—many possibilities exist. Your problems are mostly in your mind and self-created.

✦ As a card for personal growth

You are your own worst enemy. The eight of swords urges you to release self-limiting attitudes that are blocking your growth. Let go of fears and doubts; trust the Universe's plan.

Nine of Swords

✦ In questions about money

You may experience fear, negativity, guilt, sadness, or anxiety about a money matter. Losses might result because you have refused to face the truth for too long. However, these losses could lighten the burden you've been carrying. This card can also suggest you are only seeing the "downside."

✦ In questions about love

This card depicts pain caused by another person's insensitivity. You may feel lonely, rejected, or misunderstood. Perhaps you've refused to see the truth about a partner or yourself, or have allowed someone else to define you. Don't berate yourself. Be patient and try to understand where things went wrong and how you can avoid making the same mistakes in the future.

✦ In questions about work

The nine suggests that fear and negativity may be preventing your success. Perhaps you allow other people to decide what course you should take or blame them for your failures. Rather than dwelling on problems, face the truth about yourself and your objectives.

✦ As a card for personal growth

Stop seeing yourself as a victim and worrying so much about what other people think. Your negative attitudes contribute to your unhappiness. Change your perspective and you can change your life.

Ten of Swords

✦ In questions about money

The ten of swords represents a time of crisis and endings. A financial situation has reached its limit, perhaps resulting in disarray. Losses may result because you have been operating under an illusion or impropriety. However, the right action or decision can bring future success.

✦ In questions about love

The ten indicates disappointment in love. A situation has gone on as long as it can, and now you must make a change. Perhaps you have idealized your partner or a relationship, and the truth hurts. This card can also indicate that you've reached the crisis point and things will improve.

✦ In questions about work

You are overworked and exhausted. You've reached your own limits or the inevitable end of a situation. Sometimes the ten represents a crisis brought on by dishonesty, misconceptions, or overextending yourself. However, you have gained valuable knowledge through the experience—use this to make things better in the future.

✦ As a card for personal growth

The ten of swords symbolizes wisdom gained as a result of a difficult experience. You may be physically exhausted and need to take care of your health. Perhaps you are worrying too much and wearing yourself out—give it a rest.

Princess (or Page) of Swords

✦ **In questions about money**

You may receive a message or information concerning
money. This card advises you to analyze financial matters
yourself, rather than relying on someone else. Use caution.
Alternate plans may be necessary.

✦ **In questions about love**

Observe a partner or relationship carefully in order to gain
understanding. This card can also mean that someone is
watching you. The princess of swords often symbolizes an
immature, analytical, or detached approach to relationships—
perhaps you and/or a partner think and talk about love rather
than feeling it. Good communication may be needed.

✦ In questions about work

Develop confidence in your own ideas instead of naïvely following someone else's plan. In order to succeed, you may need to improve your analytical ability, skills, or education. Sometimes this card warns that someone you work with may not be trustworthy. Get to the bottom of a murky situation.

✦ As someone you know

The princess represents an aloof, cautious individual who wants to know everything about other people but doesn't reveal much about him- or herself. Although this person may have many clever and original ideas, he or she probably lacks the confidence or persistence to develop them.

✦ As a card for personal growth

You need to think for yourself and become more independent. Rather than struggling, relax, surrender, and seek understanding.

Prince (or Knight) of Swords

✦ In questions about money

You may think you know it all, but refusing to listen to others could prove costly. This card can also herald a sudden change in your income. Perhaps you need to make adjustments in your portfolio, a business venture, or another financial area. A trip concerning business or money matters is possible.

✦ In questions about love

This card often tells of a change of some kind. A new affair might begin or an existing relationship could end. Perhaps you need to change old patterns of relating, becoming more flexible and cooperative. Try not to be too critical of or harsh toward a partner.

✦ In questions about work

A change in your work environment, job, or responsibilities is likely. You may need to change your attitude or the way you perform your job, becoming more positive and open-minded. Avoid confrontation. Better focus and direction could benefit your work. This card can also represent a business trip in the near future or a job that involves travel.

✦ As someone you know

The prince symbolizes the know-it-all, a stubborn, arrogant individual who rarely takes others into account. Inquisitive and clever, he or she is impatient with people who aren't as quick mentally.

✦ As a card for personal growth

You need to change your perspective, attitude, or understanding. Rather than setting up defenses to protect your vulnerability, be more flexible and receptive.

Queen of Swords

✦ **In questions about money**

The queen of swords advises you to utilize information or communication networks/systems to generate wealth. Take control of a financial matter and turn it to your advantage. Honesty is important—don't get involved in questionable dealings or losses could result.

✦ **In questions about love**

You may feel your situation is too restrictive or bound up in tradition. Speak your mind and take a firm position if you want your needs to be met. Be truthful and forthright. Keep your emotions under control and use a detached, intellectual approach. The queen can mean you are too aloof or controlling.

✦ In questions about work

Be clear about what you want and speak up for yourself. Perhaps you feel constrained and need to exercise more control in a work-related situation. Use your intellect to produce positive results. This card can also signify a job in the field of communications or information systems.

✦ As someone you know

The queen describes an intelligent, forthright woman who knows what she wants and isn't afraid to ask for it. Although she can be too detached, even cold at times, she seeks truth, justice, and freedom from restrictive conventions.

✦ As a card for personal growth

The queen represents the triumph of intellect over emotions. Put aside sentimental or selfish feelings and be more rational and fair-minded. Take control of your destiny, rather than allowing others to decide for you.

King of Swords

✦ In questions about money

Act decisively, rather than vacillating. Use what you know to take charge of a financial matter or situation—leadership is needed. Don't reveal your information or sources at this time. Remain detached and don't let your feelings influence you. Investments involving communication fields could be profitable.

✦ In questions about love

A relationship is based on ideas, communication, or abstractions rather than deep feeling. You and/or a partner may share high ideals but interact in a cool, detached manner. Perhaps you fear you'll lose control or freedom if you fall in love. You might think and talk about love, but resist getting involved.

✦ In questions about work

The king indicates a job or career based on

communication, or intellectual pursuits. It can also advise you to show leadership and act in a decisive, dispassionate way. Focus and clarity are important. Be careful about whom you share information with. Don't give up until you get the answers you seek.

✦ As someone you know

The king usually describes a mature man who is a leader in the field of communications, law, education, or information. Intelligent and philosophical, he has high ideals and a strong sense of justice. Something of a loner, he hides his feelings and relies on his intellect.

✦ As a card for personal growth

Develop your mental powers and use knowledge to place yourself in a more commanding position. Don't let your heart rule your head. Meditate on this card to improve your intellect and/or analytical ability.

Chapter 6

Cups

The suit of cups, sometimes called chalices, describes situations involving relationships, emotions, intuition, and imagination. These cards represent the element of water. In an ordinary playing deck, cups are interpreted as hearts.

Ace of Cups

✦ In questions about money

You are about to launch a new and profitable creative endeavor. If these initial seeds of inspiration are nurtured properly, they can produce financial success. Pay attention to your intuition in a matter involving money.

✦ In questions about love

The ace heralds the start of a new relationship. It describes the early, joyful stages of a romance, when two people recognize their mutual attraction. Nurture this budding affection carefully if you want it to blossom.

✦ In questions about work

You are beginning a new project or job that you feel
passionately about. This undertaking may spark your
creativity or offer you a chance to actualize a long-held
dream. In order to maximize this opportunity, you will
have to invest effort over a period of time.

✦ As a card for personal growth

Open your heart to love, on either a personal or a spiritual
level—or both. You feel a sense of connectedness to the All
and outwardly reflect joyful feelings to others. Meditate on
this card to strengthen intuition and creativity.

Two of Cups

✦ **In questions about money**

The two of cups represents joint resources and business partnerships. A partner's abilities, capital, or connections can benefit you financially—and vice versa. By uniting your efforts, you improve your prospects so that both of you can profit.

✦ **In questions about love**

The two symbolizes the harmonious flow of affection between two people. Emotional reciprocity and an intuitive understanding of one another's needs enable you to nourish each other at a deep level. You bring out the best in one another and enjoy a happy, balanced relationship based on mutual respect, caring, and equality.

✦ In questions about work

This card describes a creative partnership in which two people merge their talents to produce an inspired outcome. By combining your abilities, you can accomplish more than you could individually. Strive to establish cooperation and equity in your workplace.

✦ As a card for personal growth

Learn the art of give-and-take. The two of cups can also symbolize the uniting of different facets of your own personality. Meditate on this card to encourage harmony and cooperation.

Three of Cups

✦ In questions about money

A collective financial venture promises good results. A card of fulfillment, the three can show you reaping rewards from an investment made with others. Use your resources for the good of your family, community, or humanity as a whole.

✦ In questions about love

It's time to share love and joy with others. The positive feelings represented by this card go beyond affection for a romantic partner and may signify a collective bond with family, friends, and kindred spirits. In some instances, the three of cups indicates a marriage or other celebration of love.

✦ In questions about work

A work-related matter should result in a positive outcome. Perhaps your good fortune will come through the collective efforts of a group. The three of cups can also show you forming a collaborative venture or celebrating your success with other people.

✦ As a card for personal growth

Learn to accept what others offer you and to share what you have with them. Resolve differences with people and encourage spiritual goodwill.

Four of Cups

✦ **In questions about money**

The four represents an emotional attachment to money. Perhaps you feel trapped by your possessions or are using money to try to satisfy emotional needs. Are you letting your emotions dictate financial matters, to your detriment? Financial stability is indicated, but not growth.

✦ **In questions about love**

A relationship lacks excitement, change, or growth. The emphasis on security and routine may be undermining your happiness. As a result, you may be bored or frustrated with your partner, yourself, and the relationship. It's time to examine your priorities and decide what you want in life.

✦ In questions about work

You feel stuck in or limited by your job. Perhaps you are placing security and comfort above all else and should reassess your priorities. You no longer feel challenged or fulfilled by your work—find something that offers you more opportunity for creative expression and growth.

✦ As a card for personal growth

The four of cups represents stagnation and boredom. Do some soul-searching to discover what you truly want and how the choices you've made have led you to this state of discontent.

Five of Cups

✦ In questions about money

The five shows disappointment and loss, although usually it is only temporary. Perhaps an investment hasn't paid off as you'd planned or you've incurred unexpected expenses. Don't throw good money after bad or lose hope. Cut your losses and move on to something better.

✦ In questions about love

A relationship hasn't lived up to your expectations. You may feel disappointed, but don't waste time on self-pity or resentment—do what's necessary to rectify the situation. A temporary separation may give you a chance to see things more clearly. The five can also mark the end of an unhappy partnership and the start of a more satisfying one.

✦ In questions about work

Your work gives you no satisfaction. Perhaps you feel your talents are being wasted or are not appreciated. Promises may not have been kept or a situation may not have turned out the way you'd expected. It's time to let go and move on to something more rewarding.

✦ As a card for personal growth

The five symbolizes a need for change and freedom. You've grown beyond your present situation and must move forward, even if it means letting go of people or things to which you have an emotional attachment.

Six of Cups

✦ **In questions about money**

The six of cups represents a connection between the past and present regarding money. A card of renewal, it can signal repayment of a debt or a return to a more financially advantageous position after a period of instability. It can also indicate financial give-and-take, or a joint venture in which you share profits and expenses with others.

✦ **In questions about love**

Joy and affection can be openly exchanged in a relationship. You are ready to show your love for a partner and your feelings are reciprocated. Obstacles disappear, enabling you to deepen your love. In some cases, the six of cups marks the return of an old lover or the reawakening of romance after a period of stalemate.

✦ In questions about work

You experience renewed enthusiasm for your work. Either the situation or your perception of it has changed, enabling you to be more creative and successful. Perhaps you've acquired new skills or knowledge that enriches your job experience or the end product. This card can mean you'll be rewarded for past efforts or that cooperation in your workplace will improve.

✦ As a card for personal growth

The six symbolizes emotional renewal and a return to happier times. You express clarity, receptivity, generosity, and creativity in all you do. Share openly and joyfully with others, knowing that your gifts will be reciprocated. Meditate on this card to increase the happiness and harmony in your life.

Seven of Cups

✦ **In questions about money**

Money matters are tinged with idealism and fantasy. You may have lots of brainstorms and come up with all sorts of moneymaking schemes, but most of these probably won't pan out. Perhaps you are being unrealistic. Some deals, investments, or plans may be mirages, so examine them carefully. Use your imagination to find inspired ways to generate income.

✦ **In questions about love**

You indulge in romantic fantasies while you try to determine what type of relationship you truly want. As you examine the many options, remember that you can't have everything and must decide what really matters. This card can also represent a highly emotional, inspired relationship that stimulates your imagination and creativity.

✦ In questions about work

Explore different career possibilities to find what's right for you. Perhaps you aren't being realistic about your vocation, skills, or future. The seven of cups may represent a job that stimulates your creativity. But a job or business opportunity that seems too good to be true should be examined closely.

✦ As a card for personal growth

Use your imagination to create the circumstances you desire in life. This card can describe a period of great inspiration and emotional exploration. Remain open to possibilities without feeling inhibited by fear or self-censorship.

Eight of Cups

✦ **In questions about money**

Concentrate on making the most of your resources. A total commitment of heart, mind, and energy is necessary if you are to prosper. Limit your investments or moneymaking activities to a few really important ones. In some cases, you may be better off abandoning something that isn't profitable.

✦ **In questions about love**

A serious relationship affects you profoundly. Be sincere and devote yourself completely to a partner. You aren't interested in casual contacts now, you want a deep and fulfilling commitment. Sometimes the eight of cups advises you to end a bad relationship that can't be salvaged.

✦ In questions about work

You pour your heart and soul into your work. Pay attention to details, do your best, and don't let anything distract you from reaching your goal. If you are willing to work for what you want, you can succeed beyond your wildest dreams. Sometimes this card recommends leaving a job you have outgrown.

✦ As a card for personal growth

Be sincere as you pursue your purpose in life. Dispense with people, activities, and distractions that take you away from your path and concentrate on the things that give your life meaning.

Nine of Cups

✦ In questions about money

The nine of cups symbolizes abundance and good fortune. Sometimes called the *wish card,* it promises success in a financial or business matter. The riches you receive will bring happiness because they result from properly applying your true self.

✦ In questions about love

You can enjoy a rich, rewarding love life. Your dreams come true with the nine of cups, whether you seek a strong and supportive, committed partnership or the excitement of many romantic liaisons. The key to happiness is knowing what you really want and opening your heart to it.

✦ In questions about work

The nine brings opportunity, rewards, and success in your career. You may find the perfect job or advance in your chosen field. Whatever you undertake now produces positive results. Wishes come true when this card appears because you are in tune with yourself and with the times.

✦ As a card for personal growth

The nine symbolizes contentment and ease. You don't have to strive or struggle—you've earned the satisfaction and peace of mind you are now experiencing. Relax and enjoy it. Meditate on this card to improve your luck.

Ten of Cups

✦ **In questions about money**

The ten heralds a time of rewards and success. Your efforts bear fruit. Financial ventures—particularly those of a collective nature—pay dividends. You achieve a position of financial security and comfort. Sometimes this card represents family money, an inheritance, or income derived from a family business.

✦ **In questions about love**

The ten of cups suggests emotional maturity and fulfillment, a supportive, loving relationship, and a lifestyle that brings you happiness. You enjoy the comfort and security that come from belonging to a family or group of like-minded individuals.

✦ In questions about work

You receive appreciation and recognition for your work. Over time, you've worked hard and proved your ability. Now you can enjoy the respect, rewards, and sense of satisfaction you deserve. The ten can also represent a collaborative venture or a job in a family business.

✦ As a card for personal growth

The ten symbolizes personal achievement, satisfaction, and self-esteem. You are comfortable with yourself and content with the life you've created. This enables you to relate to others in a mature, sincere fashion.

Princess (or Page) of Cups

✦ In questions about money

You tend to be naïve regarding financial matters. Perhaps you aren't very good at managing money or resources, or you are too trusting. This card can also show financial instability or warn that a business deal isn't clear or well founded.

✦ In questions about love

Painful experiences early in life have left you feeling vulnerable and skeptical when it comes to relationships. As a result, you may give too much of yourself or go to the opposite extreme and refuse to let anyone get close to you. Before you can enjoy a happy partnership, you need to let go of this old hurt and develop your self-esteem.

✦ In questions about work

You may be too emotionally involved in your job or connect your self-worth with your work. Perhaps you are too naïve, immature, and trusting of people. Stand up for yourself rather than letting others dominate the field. Don't leave yourself in a vulnerable position.

✦ As someone you know

The princess represents a shy, sensitive individual who lacks self-esteem and is easily hurt. This person may be too gullible and trusting or, conversely, too withdrawn and defensive. In some cases, this card describes a young person who is intuitive, creative, or spiritually inclined.

✦ As a card for personal growth

You need to strengthen your self-esteem. The princess of cups can also signify a keen intuition or natural artistic ability that can be developed to a high level.

Prince (or Knight) of Cups

✦ **In questions about money**

If your finances are stagnant, a change may bring good fortune. New opportunities could prove profitable. However, this card can also suggest that indecision, timidity, or a lack of commitment may be preventing you from realizing the rewards you desire. Sometimes the prince of cups warns that an offer or opportunity is not what it appears to be.

✦ **In questions about love**

Uncertainty or fear of commitment may prevent you from enjoying a happy relationship. Perhaps you want to keep your options open indefinitely, or you fear that a lover might hurt or dominate you if you let that person get too close. Sometimes the prince represents happiness in a romance that is free of defenses, expectations, and artifice, or a highly charged relationship with an artistic person.

✦ In questions about work

If you feel stuck in a rut, you might benefit from changing jobs. However, this card can also indicate that because you are unwilling to commit yourself to a career path, your inconsistency prevents you from getting ahead. For creative people, the prince may represent an opportunity to use your talent and imagination.

✦ As someone you know

The prince symbolizes someone who has trouble committing to anything. This person is exciting and entertaining, but tends to run away at the first sign of difficulty. You can't depend on the prince, even though he or she may have good intentions.

✦ As a card for personal growth

Face up to challenges and take some risks. Embrace new opportunities. Stop vacillating and follow things through to completion. If you make a promise, honor it.

Queen of Cups

✦ **In questions about money**

Use your intuition in business and financial deals, but don't ignore common sense and practicality. You may need to be flexible during a time when circumstances are in flux. For artistic individuals, this card suggests that you can profit from your creativity.

✦ **In questions about love**

The queen represents unconditional love, nurturing, and acceptance. Don't judge others or expect them to fulfill your wishes. Be flexible in matters of the heart. Sometimes this card says you need to be more discriminating in your choice of partners—allow them to be themselves, but not at your expense.

✦ **In questions about work**

You can use your imagination and creativity to produce

inspired work of high quality, infusing everything you do with beauty. Changes in your workplace or career path are possible. Be flexible in work-related matters. In some cases, this card represents a job or field that focuses on women.

✦ As someone you know

The queen describes a highly emotional, creative, intuitive individual, usually a woman. She is receptive and loving, refusing to pass judgment. Ruled by her feelings, she seeks pleasure and may be changeable or unreliable. This card can also symbolize a nurturing, compassionate person who opens her home and heart to all who seek comfort.

✦ As a card for personal growth

Develop your feminine side, whether you are male or female. Perhaps you need to become more compassionate and accepting. Meditate on this card to strengthen your intuition and imagination.

King of Cups

✦ **In questions about money**

Your emotions may be influencing your financial dealings and business matters. Take control of situations involving money, resources, investments, or property, but be considerate of others. Your chances of success increase if you devote yourself 100 percent to a venture.

✦ **In questions about love**

Commitment, loyalty, and trust are needed. Although you desire a relationship, you or a partner might be afraid to express feelings for fear of losing control. The king of cups can also indicate manipulation, secretiveness, or defensiveness in romantic situations. On the positive side, it can symbolize emotional maturity and an ability to nurture, protect, and empathize with a partner.

✦ In questions about work

The king shows a desire for control, which can result in power struggles. You or someone you work with may be self-righteous, territorial, or overly protective due to a fear of losing ground to someone else. This card recommends that you assist others. Use your intuition and creativity to further your career.

✦ As someone you know

The king represents an emotionally controlled—and controlling—man who shuns relationships or tries to manipulate romantic situations in order to retain a sense of power. Although he has deep feelings, he has trouble expressing them. In some cases, this card signifies the "wounded healer" who tries to work out his own problems by helping others. It can also show a spiritual person who seeks Divine Love instead of personal love.

✦ As a card for personal growth

Learn to trust others and be receptive to them. Revealing yourself doesn't necessarily place you in a vulnerable position. Meditate on this card to become more open and accepting.

Chapter 7

Wands

The suit of wands, sometimes called rods or staves, describes situations involving creativity, action, willpower, enthusiasm, spirituality, and self-confidence. These cards represent the element of fire. In an ordinary playing deck, clubs are the equivalent of wands.

Ace of Wands

✦ **In questions about money**

The ace shows an initial investment in a creative endeavor. You may start to earn money from something you feel passionately about. Seek new adventures and opportunities. Trust your instincts and be creative in handling financial matters.

✦ **In questions about love**

This card often represents the beginning of a passionate new romance or a burst of enthusiasm in an existing relationship. A partner may spark your imagination and creativity. Act on your feelings—don't wait for the other person to make the first move. A positive response from a lover is likely.

✦ In questions about work

An opportunity that engages your imagination and talents could come your way. Now is the time to put your heart and soul into a project, job, or business venture. Embrace new experiences that come your way. Success is possible, but you must be willing to invest the energy necessary to make it happen. Optimism and self-confidence are important assets.

✦ As a card for personal growth

The ace depicts a time of new experiences and potential for growth. Your creative energy is awakening, along with your confidence. Open yourself joyfully to new challenges and opportunities.

Two of Wands

✦ **In questions about money**

Take command of financial matters and learn to make it on your own. Be confident. Although you may opt to accept someone else's assistance, don't rely on outside support that compromises your self-worth, principles, or control.

✦ **In questions about love**

The two symbolizes the stage in the development of a relationship when both people must declare themselves and begin structuring the partnership. With vision and enthusiasm, you can build a rewarding relationship. This card can also signify a creative partnership in which each person inspires the other.

✦ In questions about work

Invest energy and drive in your work. It's time to put your
plans into action. Take control of your work situation and
pursue your ambitions passionately—don't let anything stand
in your way. Embrace challenges that stretch your capabilities
rather than settling for comfort, ease, and security.

✦ As a card for personal growth

Clearly define your goals, principles, territory, or purpose.
Don't sit passively while life goes on all around you—
get involved. Use your willpower to bring your dreams
to fruition.

Three of Wands

✦ **In questions about money**

Publicize yourself and promote your efforts in order to increase profits. You must take charge, be energetic, and make it happen. Your enthusiasm and confidence can inspire others and contribute to the success of a financial matter.

✦ **In questions about love**

It's time to demonstrate your affection honestly, openly, and passionately. Let your partner know how much you care. Celebrate your love. In some cases, this card can show marriage or another form of commitment that recognizes and honors your partnership.

✦ In questions about work

Express your creativity in a wholehearted, joyful manner. This can be an exciting time, during which you invest a lot of creative energy in a project and your talents are recognized. You may need to be flexible or collaborate with others in order to succeed. Integrity is important.

✦ As a card for personal growth

The three represents a period of passionate involvement in life. Your inspiration and creativity are awakened. Devote yourself to developing your ideas. Whatever you put your heart and soul into will bring you pleasure and perhaps inspire others.

Four of Wands

✦ In questions about money

Getting this card suggests that you'll enjoy financial ease and stability. This is a good time to seek financial backing. The four indicates that an investment, business, or other money matter should work out in your favor. Now is the time to reap the rewards due to you.

✦ In questions about love

The four of wands signals happiness, stability, and harmony in a relationship. Romance is in the air. Past problems can now be resolved. Because you know what you want and feel positive about yourself, you can attract someone who is right for you.

✦ In questions about work

Success and contentment come after a period of hard work. A project or job undertaken now is likely to provide comfort and fulfillment. Pay attention to details and be sure to follow through. This card can also symbolize the successful completion of a project and the satisfaction that comes from a job well done.

✦ As a card for personal growth

The four of wands represents a time of peace, contentment, and comfort. You feel good about yourself and your place in life, knowing you've earned your happiness. Share your experience with others.

Five of Wands

✦ In questions about money

Disputes arise over resources, property, ideas, rights, or territory. Confusion or disagreements may exist about how to make, use, invest, or spend money. Be practical—losses may result if you don't pay attention to what's going on around you. Don't seek financial advice from others or begin a legal matter involving money or property at this time.

✦ In questions about love

Petty matters cause squabbles between you and a partner. Ego battles flare up, but nothing gets resolved. Both of you are probably being selfish, stubbornly holding on to your positions and refusing to see the other person's side. Be more flexible and cooperative.

✦ In questions about work

Arguments, confusion, and disarray disrupt your work environment or career path. Egotism and stubbornness interfere with progress. Perhaps you are being too idealistic, ignoring practical or financial matters to your detriment.

✦ As a card for personal growth

Put aside ego issues and entrenched behaviors that are keeping you from moving forward. This card can also indicate that you have your head in the clouds and need to deal with "real world" concerns.

Six of Wands

✦ **In questions about money**

Success and financial gains can now be yours, perhaps after a period of hard work or struggle. In legal matters and business ventures, this card indicates victory. An investment, particularly a long-term one or one that has involved some risk, should pay off.

✦ **In questions about love**

The six signals a time of happiness, peace, and cooperation. You and a partner overcome difficulties and enjoy good times together. You are ready to express your feelings ardently and openly, perhaps through marriage or another form of commitment. If you are looking for love, you stand a good chance of finding it now.

✦ In questions about work

You enjoy success and satisfaction in your work. Getting this card can mean you will win a victory, land the perfect job, or achieve excellence in a challenging endeavor. This is a time for action and advancement. You reap the rewards that are due to you and receive the recognition you deserve.

✦ As a card for personal growth

This is a period of joy and accomplishment. You've been tested and have met the challenge. Victory is yours. The six of wands can also represent recovery from an illness or injury. Meditate on this card to attract success and happiness in life.

Seven of Wands

✦ **In questions about money**

Stick with a financial venture, plan, or course of action, even though things may seem difficult at present. In order to profit, you might have to invest a good deal of effort. Stand your ground, but don't get into a conflict over money or possessions at this time.

✦ **In questions about love**

Do what's necessary to make a relationship work. Difficulties can be resolved, but it may take some time and effort. Don't give up hope. Stay positive and involved, even though it seems easier just to quit trying.

✦ In questions about work

Keep your enthusiasm high and continue to work hard to achieve your goals. Set priorities and invest energy where it will do the most good. Persevere—you can succeed, but it may take time. Don't let disappointments, other people, or distractions keep you from reaching your objective.

✦ As a card for personal growth

The seven of wands symbolizes the growth that comes through effort, diligence, and patience. You must be willing to work for what you want. Disperse negative attitudes that weaken your resolve and avoid people who bring you down.

Eight of Wands

✦ **In questions about money**

The eight heralds a time of excitement, urgency, and rapid developments. You may have to act or make decisions quickly. Expect opportunities, information, or results to come soon. *Carpe diem!*

✦ **In questions about love**

This card represents passion and excitement. A love affair may begin suddenly and sweep you off your feet, or the fire might flare up in an existing relationship. Spontaneous actions, such as a hasty marriage, are sometimes indicated by the eight of wands.

✦ In questions about work

You undergo a busy period when matters develop suddenly and you must think, act, and make decisions quickly. During this exciting time you feel inspired and creative, as well as challenged. You can make rapid progress now and your career could accelerate. A business trip is possible.

✦ As a card for personal growth

This is a time for action. Be daring, take a few risks, and try something new that you've always wanted to do. Follow your bliss.

Nine of Wands

✦ In questions about money

The nine of wands represents financial security and stability. If you have suffered losses in the past, this card signals a recovery. However, you may still have to wait a while before you achieve a position of unassailable strength and your assets reach a peak. Hang in there—your position is strong enough to weather challenges.

✦ In questions about love

The "silver lining" card, the nine of wands promises better days ahead. It can mean that you and a partner resolve your difficulties, or that if the relationship ends, you will emerge stronger. The nine may also advise you to be patient rather than pushing for immediate results.

✦ In questions about work

You have the resilience and ability to rebound from setbacks. Continue working toward your goal, for even if you feel discouraged, the worst is over. Success and security lie ahead. Temporary delays give you a chance to strengthen your position. Stand your ground in the face of adversity.

✦ As a card for personal growth

Your troubles are behind you. You have overcome challenges and are much stronger as a result. This card can also show recovery after an illness or injury.

Ten of Wands

✦ **In questions about money**

Money issues may be weighing you down. Perhaps other people rely on you for support or your financial situation impacts others, so you must continue to carry the burden. The ten can also suggest that you are too preoccupied with money and need to shift your perspective.

✦ **In questions about love**

The ten represents a mature and responsible attitude toward relationships. You take love seriously and feel a commitment to your partner. Sometimes this card shows marriage or a strong, lasting bond between two people who care deeply about each other. It can also symbolize a relationship that demands a lot of you.

✦ In questions about work

You have more responsibility or work than you can comfortably handle. You feel burdened, but can't set down your load yet, perhaps because other people depend on you. Try to delegate duties and authority to relieve stress. Although the challenges you're laboring under are exhausting, they will push you to learn and grow stronger.

✦ As a card for personal growth

The ten of wands is a card of exhaustion. You have taken on too much and need to give yourself a break. If that isn't possible, find a way to improve your ability to handle the responsibility or duties you're charged with.

Princess (or Page) of Wands

✦ **In questions about money**

A venture or investment has potential, but it is not yet
fully developed. Take a creative approach in handling your
money matters.

✦ **In questions about love**

This card symbolizes enthusiasm, openness, and optimism
in love. A relationship is based on mutual affection, loyalty,
and honesty. Open your heart and give yourself entirely to
a partner.

✦ **In questions about work**

The princess can represent a job or opportunity that offers
you the potential for creative expression and excitement.
Although you may not get "top billing," if you develop
your talents and skills, you can progress. See this as a step

in the right direction. Don't let other people discourage you from doing what you enjoy.

✦ As someone you know

The princess represents a youthful, lively, and entertaining person of either sex. A loyal companion, he or she expresses feelings openly and ardently. Like a child, the princess lives for the moment and enjoys being the center of attention.

✦ As a card for personal growth

Connect with the fun-loving side of yourself, the child within. Approach life with joy and hope, seeking truth, love, and beauty in all things.

Prince (or Knight) of Wands

✦ In questions about money

The prince of wands is a card of change. It can advise you to let go of an investment, property, business, or other financial matter and move on to something else—a better opportunity may be on the horizon. Sometimes this card indicates that you are too attached to money and possessions. Be daring—fear of risk and change may be limiting your prosperity.

✦ In questions about love

This card shows a lack of commitment or constancy. You or a partner may desire freedom and shun responsibility. A love affair may be fun and exciting, but don't expect it to last. In some cases, the prince of wands represents leaving a relationship that lacks passion. Perhaps you need to be more adventurous in the game of love.

✦ In questions about work

A job change, relocation, or shift in responsibilities is likely. It's time to challenge yourself and take a few risks. A business trip may be in the offing. Sometimes this card says you aren't using your talents fully or that you need to be more creative, assertive, and unconventional.

✦ As someone you know

The prince describes a changeable person who abhors commitment, responsibility, and conventions. A free spirit, he or she is always in pursuit of adventure. This card may also symbolize an agent of change in your life.

✦ As a card for personal growth

It's time for a change. Perhaps you need to be more adventurous and less conservative. If you've gotten in a rut, this card recommends shaking things up a bit. It can also mean a trip is in your future.

Queen of Wands

✦ In questions about money

Apply your talents and imagination productively—do what you love and the money will follow. This card may also advise you to be astute and to take control of financial matters. You may be able to help others prosper, too.

✦ In questions about love

This card describes a passionate romance in which both partners openly express their deep feelings. You know what you want—go for it. Loyalty, ardor, and devotion are strong factors in the relationship, but jealousy can be a problem.

✦ In questions about work

Channel all your energy and enthusiasm into a job, business, or project if you want it to bear fruit. Success is likely, but direct, assertive measures are needed. Stand up for what you believe. Other people might benefit from your encouragement.

✦ As someone you know

The queen is usually an outspoken, passionate, dramatic woman who likes to rule, but is never ruled. A loyal friend, she stands behind the people she cares about. Often she is a creative individual who inspires others to do their best.

✦ As a card for personal growth

Follow your dreams. Don't let anyone else tell you how you should live your life.

King of Wands

✦ **In questions about money**

Integrity and steadfastness are necessary in financial matters. This card may describe an ambitious venture that promises success, but will require a great deal of energy and dedication. It can also mean financial support is available or that a partner is trustworthy.

✦ **In questions about love**

The king of wands describes a lively, warm, and loving relationship between two people who are dedicated to one another. Loyalty is important. Don't expect someone who is already attached to leave his or her mate. This card can also suggest showing your feelings without reservation.

✦ In questions about work

This is the card of the leader; when it appears, it tells you to take charge, display leadership ability, and inspire trust in others. Be decisive and ambitious. Your efforts and talents have a good chance of being recognized now. Involvement in a creative project or a worthy cause is possible.

✦ As someone you know

The king is an acknowledged leader with high ideals and a passionate spirit. Usually a mature man, he is strong, confident, and energetic. He encourages the people around him, inspiring their trust and loyalty.

✦ As a card for personal growth

Be courageous, decisive, and creative. Live your ideals. Approach life with passion and confidence. If you treat others with respect and loyalty, they'll reciprocate in kind.

Chapter 8

The Major Arcana

Early tarot decks may have contained only the twenty-two cards of the major arcana, which are known as "trumps." Often this portion of the tarot is viewed as a journey from innocence (The Fool) to wisdom (The World), with each card representing a step on the road to enlightenment.

When a card from the major arcana appears in a reading, it suggests that destiny or other forces beyond the individual's control are at work in the matter. If several trumps turn up in a spread, the situation may seem "fated."

0: The Fool

✦ In questions about money

You may be immature or naïve when it comes to handling money. If you are considering an investment, examine matters carefully, pay attention to details, and make sure you have all the information you need. The Fool can also represent the first stage of a financial endeavor or business opportunity.

✦ In questions about love

Unforeseen circumstances may have brought you a relationship that seems "fated." Approach this association with innocence, trust, and an open heart. Be spontaneous and joyful as you enter into a new romance or a new stage of an existing partnership.

✦ In questions about work

The Fool represents the start of a new job, career path, or business venture. Go into this situation with an open mind and a positive attitude, embracing opportunities as they present themselves. You have much to learn—pay attention.

✦ As a person you know

The Fool symbolizes someone who is a child at heart, playful, trusting, and innocent. This individual doesn't view life very seriously and may not be particularly dependable. He or she takes things as they come, blissfully unaware of dangers or obstacles lying ahead in the journey of life.

✦ As a card for personal growth

You are beginning a journey and it may take some time to reach your destination. Let yourself be guided by your inner knowing and Fate. Experience is a great teacher and you could be in for some surprises along the way. Keep an open mind and trust that things will work out for the best. Don't worry, be happy!

1: The Magician

✦ **In questions about money**

Take charge of money matters so you are in control of your financial situation. You have the power to generate money by using your talents wisely. Tap into the universal flow to increase your wealth. This card can also suggest that you or someone else is working behind the scenes or using hidden resources to profit.

✦ **In questions about love**

 Control, manipulation, or issues of power may be at work in a relationship. Perhaps you are engaged in a power struggle in which one or both of you are playing games. Rather than stubbornly trying to gain an advantage, seek a win–win situation.

✦ **In questions about work**

Someone may secretly be working to gain power and control, or manipulating a situation to get what he or she wants.

Hidden issues as yet unknown to you may exist. Power struggles are likely. Watch your back and don't get involved in anything questionable. Don't reveal everything you know.

✦ As a person you know

The Magician represents someone who is secretive, private, and perhaps untrustworthy. This person prefers to work behind the scenes, manipulating circumstances to gain power and control. He or she might be a trickster who takes advantage of situations and people. In a positive sense, this card may indicate someone who has highly developed psychic or magical powers.

✦ As a card for personal growth

Take control of your life and your environment rather than allowing someone else to have power over you. Align yourself with Divine Will and tap the energy of the Universe to create the circumstances you desire.

2: The High Priestess

✦ **In questions about money**

Trust your intuition in a financial matter. This card can also suggest that you are too "otherworldly" and could benefit from becoming more practical about handling money and possessions.

✦ **In questions about love**

Your instincts about a relationship or a partner are probably correct. Listen to your heart and be guided by your feelings, rather than trying to analyze a person or romantic situation too closely.

✦ **In questions about work**

Listen to your inner voice and let it guide you in work-related decisions. Don't rely totally on practical solutions or rational analyses—trust your hunches, too. The High Priestess can also be a signal to look at the inner dimensions of a matter rather than accepting things at face value.

✦ As a person you know

The High Priestess represents an intuitive individual or one who has access to esoteric or spiritual knowledge. This person may be rather solitary or reclusive, perhaps because he or she is too sensitive to cope with the stress of an active, public life.

✦ As a card for personal growth

Look inward and pay attention to your intuition. Work at developing your natural abilities and your spiritual side.

3: The Empress

✦ In questions about money

The Empress represents the wise management of money and material resources. You may be able to benefit from a partnership or group endeavor. Good fortune and financial security are indicated. This card can also suggest that you need to value your abilities more highly or improve your sense of self-worth.

✦ In questions about love

The Empress describes a mature attitude toward relationships. You aren't frivolous with your love and seek a partnership based on respect, trust, deep affection, and give-and-take. You are sincere in your feelings and willing to make a commitment to a partner. In a man's reading, the Empress can represent a strong, loyal, and accomplished mate who fits his romantic ideal.

✦ In questions about work

Creative partnerships could be advantageous to you—teamwork is called for at this time. Use your talents wisely and responsibly to benefit yourself and others. Do your best and apply creativity in executing a job or project.

✦ As a person you know

The Empress represents a mature, self-confident, productive person, usually a woman. This individual is often creative and inspired. She eagerly supports the efforts of others and is a source of strength to the people she knows.

✦ As a card for personal growth

The Empress represents feminine power and reminds you to develop your feminine side, regardless of whether you are male or female. Meditate on this card to stimulate creativity, inspiration, and emotional balance.

4: The Emperor

✦ In questions about money

Manage your finances wisely to make certain your situation is stable and secure. Be efficient and practical as you aggressively pursue your goals. You might be entrusted with money and/or material resources in a business, legal matter, estate, or other venture. You have the potential to be successful in financial areas.

✦ In questions about love

The Emperor symbolizes a mature and practical approach to relationships. Sometimes it shows a relationship based mainly on material or practical considerations. In a woman's reading, this card can indicate a male partner who is stable, financially secure, and mature, but perhaps emotionally undemonstrative.

✦ In questions about work

Put emphasis on organization, responsibility, and order.

Develop stability and structure in your work environment. A business plan or efficient system may be required. You might have to take responsibility for other people or assume the role of leader. This card can also represent a job in business, law, finance, or management.

✦ As a person you know

The Emperor represents someone in a position of authority, usually a mature man, perhaps a father figure. Generally the card indicates a practical person who is a good manager, a businessman, or someone who works in a financial field. A strong, stable individual, he can be relied upon to give good advice, support your efforts, or further your progress.

✦ As a card for personal growth

Be more practical and responsible. Meditate on this card to strengthen your sense of self-worth, increase confidence, and become more grounded in the physical/material world.

5: The Hierophant

✦ In questions about money

Use your knowledge to earn money, but you'll probably have to abide by established rules and regulations. Perhaps you need to examine your attitudes about money—do you feel that having money isn't spiritual? The Hierophant can also mean that you should be paying attention to higher truths rather than focusing on material concerns.

✦ In questions about love

The Hierophant symbolizes the highest, spiritual dimensions of a relationship. You and your partner may share an inspired goal or be devoted to a higher cause. Your relationship brings out the best in both of you. This card can signify personal love as a spiritual quest or path to Divine Love. It may also indicate marriage or a stable partnership with clearly defined limits.

✦ In questions about work

You may have to play by the rules or operate within an existing structure to get ahead. The Hierophant can signify working in a field that involves knowledge, religion, or long-standing traditions. It may also advise you to combine your spiritual path with a career.

✦ As a person you know

The Hierophant is a recognized authority or leader, often a teacher or someone in a spiritual field. This person may be in a position to interpret laws, traditions, religious or cultural beliefs. Often he or she is someone you can look to for guidance.

✦ As a card for personal growth

You are learning a lesson the hard way. Wisdom is born of experience, and the great truths in life often come as a result of difficulty and suffering. Meditate on the card to learn the purpose of a challenge.

6: The Lovers

✦ In questions about money

You might profit by allying yourself with a business partner.
Perhaps a spouse or lover's resources could benefit you.
This card can also mean you'll receive financial backing for
a project or venture. The Lovers signals good fortune,
especially in cooperative endeavors.

✦ In questions about love

This card depicts a mutually rewarding relationship. You
and your partner enjoy a harmonious, joyful union that
brings out the best in both of you. Sometimes the Lovers
advises you to make a choice in a love matter.

✦ In questions about work

Joint ventures, teamwork, and partnerships are advised.
Don't try to go it alone. Combine creativity with

pragmatism. Sometimes this card suggests that you need to be more cooperative and less selfish or competitive.

✦ As a person you know

The Lovers often represents a romantic partner. It may also signify someone who possesses qualities you lack and who can complement you. Sometimes this card symbolizes a person who resolves differences and brings people together—a marriage counselor, mediator, or agent.

✦ As a card for personal growth

This card can suggest a time of harmony and balance, when your inner and outer nature are functioning in tandem. Meditate on The Lovers to help unite the masculine and feminine parts of your personality.

7: The Chariot

✦ **In questions about money**

You can't rush things. An investment may need time to grow or it may take a while for a financial situation to improve. Tend to related matters in the meantime and use your energy productively. This card may also advise you to take the reins and control the forces operating at this time.

✦ **In questions about love**

This may not be the right time for a relationship, or the right person hasn't come into your life yet. Don't despair. Perhaps you need to spend time in self-development or doing other things before immersing yourself in a partnership. This card can also advise you to focus on your path.

✦ **In questions about work**

Be patient and wait until the time is right to make your

move. Don't try to push things to develop prematurely. Take this opportunity to acquire skills, knowledge, or experience. Harness your energy and focus on your goal. By reining in your ambition and impatience, you gain power. Watch and listen carefully while you wait—later on, you can use what you learn during this period to your advantage.

✦ As a person you know

The Chariot may represent someone who holds the reins or is in a position of power. This person might control your life at this time.

✦ As a card for personal growth

The Chariot recommends patience and detachment. Don't worry about how things will unfold, just trust that you will reach your destination at the proper time. Learn all you can during this time of gestation. Direct your power constructively.

8: Strength

✦ **In questions about money**

Overcome obstacles and fears that are keeping you from being prosperous. Stop relying on others and start earning your own way. You possess the inner resources to become financially successful—use them.

✦ **In questions about love**

Be strong and persevering, even though things seem difficult. Someone you care about may challenge you to change your usual way of relating. You may be required to give up your defenses, self-limiting attitudes, and old habits. Overcome your ego, doubts, and fears in order to achieve happiness and harmony.

✦ **In questions about work**

In order to succeed, you may have to confront deep-seated fears or beliefs that are standing in your way. Be ruthless in dealing with these issues. If you overcome your weaknesses, you will go far. A challenging work-related matter might require you to draw on your inner strength. Hang in there.

✦ As a person you know

Strength describes someone who possesses inner strength, self-confidence, tenacity, and fearlessness in the face of adversity. This person doesn't need to use outward force to make a point—he or she leads by example and inspires confidence in others.

✦ As a card for personal growth

Negativity and/or old habits may be holding you back. It's time to stand on your own two feet and overcome self-imposed limitations. Meditate on this card to strengthen your self-confidence, determination, and courage.

9: The Hermit

✦ In questions about money

Learn to live on your own and become more independent. This card could signal a period of withdrawal from the material world in order to focus on your inner life or spiritual path. Money may not seem very important to you now. The Hermit may also tell you to let go of your attachment to a financial issue.

✦ In questions about love

Being alone for a time could help you to develop your ideas, talents, or self-reliance. You may not feel like socializing or being with a partner, preferring a solitary existence instead. Even if you are in a relationship, your focus is on yourself and your own path now.

✦ In questions about work

You need independence in order to develop yourself and

discover what really matters to you. Rather than working for a company or organization, this card may recommend freelancing or self-employment. The Hermit can also mean that you need to take some time off.

✦ As a person you know

The Hermit is a loner, a solitary type who lives by his or her own rules. This person is not dependent on others and does not seek their approval. The Hermit's philosophy of life has been honed through personal experience and soul-searching.

✦ As a card for personal growth

Withdraw from the activity of the world around you and look inward. You need to discover your own truth, and often the only way to do this is through enforced solitude, meditation, and simplifying your life. Even if you can't drop all your responsibilities, carve out some time for yourself.

10: The Wheel of Fortune

✦ In questions about money

Things are on the upswing. Your finances should improve soon, perhaps through what seems to be a stroke of luck. Opportunities may come your way simply because you are in the right place at the right time.

✦ In questions about love

Your love life is about to improve. An existing relationship gets better or a new romance comes into your life. You don't have to do anything to attract the good luck heralded by The Wheel of Fortune, it occurs because the time is right.

✦ In questions about work

You could get a lucky break. Good fortune comes unexpectedly or in a way that seems fortuitous rather than planned. A challenging work situation becomes easier or events turn in your favor without any effort on your part.

✦ As a person you know

This card may represent someone who brings you good luck or opens doors for you. You may meet this person in an unexpected way, and the encounter might seem fated.

✦ As a card for personal growth

This card represents the cyclic nature of life and recommends putting yourself in harmony with the ebb and flow of the Universe. Don't try to control things too much. Have faith that all is taken care of and will unfold according to a cosmic plan.

11: Justice

✦ In questions about money

This card symbolizes a fair and equitable division of wealth. Justice may mean that a legal matter involving money or property will be decided in your favor, if it is rightfully yours. In some cases, a payback may be called for. Acquire wealth through honest means and use it for the greater good rather than to benefit only a few.

✦ In questions about love

A more equitable arrangement may be necessary. Fair play, honesty, and consideration are called for in a relationship. One of you may be required to right a wrong or adjust your behavior to create balance and peace.

✦ In questions about work

Balance, fairness, and honesty are needed in your work arena.

Perhaps more equitable divisions of labor and responsibility are in order. Justice can also point to a time when problems are resolved and tensions abate. In some instances, it may symbolize a matter that must be handled by the courts.

✦ As a person you know

Justice may represent a lawyer, judge, or other person involved in the legal system. It can also stand for someone who mediates disputes, keeps the peace, or makes things run smoothly. This person generally is honest and fair-minded, able to see other people's viewpoints as well as his or her own.

✦ As a card for personal growth

Settle disputes, right wrongs, and adjust your conduct so you become more kind, considerate, and selfless. Try to achieve balance in all areas of your life. Take other people into consideration. Meditate on this card to bring about peace and harmony.

12: The Hanged Man

✦ **In questions about money**

The Hanged Man often represents a sacrifice or loss of some kind. You may need to cut your losses or give up something secure that prevents you from moving forward. Sometimes this card advises you to turn away from a materialistic lifestyle to pursue higher values. If the way you've been doing things is no longer profitable, this card says it's time for a change.

✦ **In questions about love**

A change of some kind is necessary. Relinquish control. You may need to sacrifice egoistic tendencies and desires for the good of the partnership. Or, depending on circumstances, you might be better off giving up a relationship that is no longer right for you.

✦ In questions about work

A 180-degree shift is in order. Rather than following the usual course of action, you need to radically change the way you do things: Out with the old, in with the new. Perhaps it's time to look for a new job or give up a secure situation in favor of something more challenging and rewarding.

✦ As a person you know

The Hanged Man may appear as someone who rejects the status quo and marches to the beat of a different drummer. The material world may not matter to this person. This card can also represent someone who acts as an agent for change in your life.

✦ As a card for personal growth

Let go of old, limiting ideas or behaviors in order to adopt more positive, beneficial ones. Meditate on this card to become more trusting and less controlling.

13: Death

✦ In questions about money

A major change is about to occur or is necessary at this time. This card may signal the end of one financial endeavor and the start of another. Old conditions, investments, or ways of handling money matters must die to make room for new growth.

✦ In questions about love

If a relationship is no longer satisfying, it is time to end things and seek a more fulfilling partnership. Death can also advise you to change the way you relate to a partner, giving up old attitudes and behaviors in favor of ones that inspire growth.

✦ In questions about work

The Death card may show the end of a job or career path, or a major shift in your work situation. If your current occupation is too limiting, consider moving on to something more challenging and rewarding.

✦ As a person you know

Death symbolizes someone who transforms you, perhaps by helping you to leave behind an old way of life for something new. It can also show someone who is moving out of your life. In some instances, this card may represent a person who is involved with death and regeneration, such as a building renovator, surgeon, or funeral director.

✦ As a card for personal growth

You need to shed ideas, behaviors, a lifestyle, or people that are hindering your growth. It's time to let a part of your self or an old way of life die so that something better can rise from the ashes. Meditating on this card can help you through a transition or loss.

14: Temperance

✦ **In questions about money**

Moderation is in order. Avoid extremes and balance spending with saving money. Take care of outstanding debts. A joint financial venture could prove beneficial. This card can also signify a period when your financial situation is balanced.

✦ **In questions about love**

Heal old wounds and establish harmony in a relationship. Avoid ego battles and power struggles, and allow love to unfold in a gradual, peaceful manner. Balance, acceptance, and equality are important now.

✦ **In questions about work**

Balance work and play so that your life becomes well rounded. This card also may show a need to make peace with coworkers, clients, or colleagues. Distribute responsibility equally in your workplace. Avoid power struggles and don't be overly ambitious at this time.

✦ As a person you know

Temperance may represent someone who is a peacemaker or mediator, someone who resolves differences and solves problems. This card can also signify a person who is well balanced, compassionate, and at peace with him- or herself.

✦ As a card for personal growth

Avoid extremes of any kind and moderate your behavior. Seek a more peaceful and balanced existence. Try to be more forgiving, kind, and fair with others—and yourself. Meditate on this card to reduce stress and restore harmony.

15: The Devil

✦ **In questions about money**

You may be too attached to money and material things. In your drive to acquire wealth, you might be losing sight of other areas that are important, too. Are you profiting at someone else's expense? If so, this card advises you to reassess your values.

✦ **In questions about love**

An obsession, a fixation, or a desire may be so strong that it interferes with your ability to see a person or situation clearly. The Devil also can describe a destructive relationship or a partner who isn't good for you but whom you stay with because you are unwilling to make a change.

✦ **In questions about work**

This is the card of the workaholic. You may be so caught up in your career that you neglect other areas of life.

Perhaps you stay in a job you hate because you're afraid to make a change. In some cases, the Devil warns that you or someone else is involved in questionable practices.

✦ As a person you know

The Devil represents someone who controls, undermines, intimidates, or brings out the worst in you. It can also show your own "shadow" side or inner demons, the part of you that you don't acknowledge.

✦ As a card for personal growth

You may be controlled by obsessions, fears, and powerful emotions. Meditate on The Devil to understand the psychological conditions that are making you unhappy, or to release attachments to unhealthy factors in your life.

16: The Tower

✦ In questions about money

A major change in your finances is about to take place. This shake-up will occur unexpectedly and may result in a loss of money or possessions. As your false sense of security crumbles, however, you feel free of responsibilities, and limitations.

✦ In questions about love

The Tower signifies a breakup or transformation in a relationship. Illusions you may have held about a partner or yourself could be shattered, allowing you to see things more clearly. Although this sudden change may cause pain, in the end you will welcome the freedom that results.

✦ In questions about work

You could be in for a shock or unexpected change in your job situation. This upset may shake your foundations or threaten your sense of security. However, The Tower indicates that transformation is necessary. Old structures must be destroyed so you can find greater independence and freedom of expression.

✦ As a person you know

The Tower symbolizes someone who serves as an agent for change in your life. He or she may come into your life unexpectedly and leave just as suddenly. This person awakens you to the truth and forces you to release your illusions.

✦ As a card for personal growth

The Tower shocks you into seeing how you have been deluding yourself by shattering the protective barriers you've established to make yourself comfortable. Embrace the changes and freedom that come, rather than trying to hold onto false securities. Meditating on The Tower can help you through a stressful transformation.

17: The Star

✦ In questions about money

Be hopeful, for your expectations can be realized. One of
the most positive cards in the major arcana, The Star
promises improvement in your financial situation. You
may have to work hard to accomplish your aims, but your
efforts will be rewarded.

✦ In questions about love

Your dreams of happiness are about to come true. Although
you still may need to do some work building or refining a
relationship, The Star tells you to remain hopeful—things
will get better.

✦ In questions about work

You may soon be a "star" and attract accolades in your job
or field of expertise. Now is the time to work hard to bring

your dreams to fruition. Hold onto your ideals and strive to do your best. Obstacles can be overcome. Success is just around the corner.

✦ As a person you know

The Star can represent someone with "star" quality who attracts attention wherever he or she goes. An association with this person might help you to move into the spotlight or improve your chances for success.

✦ As a card for personal growth

The Star urges you to be hopeful—don't give up your ideals. You are capable of achieving even your wildest dreams. If you feel discouraged or are experiencing challenges in your life, meditate on this card to improve your confidence.

18: The Moon

✦ **In questions about money**

Some facets of a financial matter are unclear—hidden conditions may exist. Don't get involved in questionable investments or dealings at this time. Financial ups and downs are possible. For creative people, The Moon may represent earning money through artistic endeavors.

✦ **In questions about love**

A deep, idealistic connection exists between two individuals. Other people may not understand your attraction—even you might not be able to explain what's going on. Sometimes this card describes a clandestine affair. It can also indicate a volatile relationship with many emotional highs and lows.

✦ In questions about work

Look more deeply into a work situation or vocational choice. Hidden matters might be about to come to light. A situation may be in transition. Perhaps you hold illusions about your work or need to be more realistic about your capabilities. The Moon can also recommend being more imaginative in your job.

✦ As a person you know

The Moon may represent an artist or highly imaginative individual. It can also describe someone who deals with psychological or hidden issues. This person might stir up your dark side, probe your secrets, or touch you at a deep level.

✦ As a card for personal growth

Get in touch with your subconscious and any fears, blocks, memories, or secret issues you need to address. Meditate on this card to connect with your hidden side or spark your imagination.

19: The Sun

✦ **In questions about money**

Brighter days lie ahead. Financial problems pale, confusion disappears, and you see how to make the most of your resources. This card bodes well for investments or business ventures.

✦ **In questions about love**

This card symbolizes contentment, openness, and a strong bond between two people. You share something special and can bring out the best in each other. The Sun's bright light enables you to see one another and the relationship clearly.

✦ **In questions about work**

You are in control and using your abilities advantageously. You clearly see your goal and how to achieve it. Success, rewards, and recognition are likely to come your way. You can also serve as an inspiration to others and help them in their work.

✦ As a person you know

The Sun symbolizes a capable, confident person who lights the way for others. A positive force in your life, he or she is someone worthy of respect. This individual may be a leader, a creative person, or someone who helps you see things more clearly.

✦ As a card for personal growth

The Sun encourages you to be happy and spread joy to others. Take control of circumstances in your life and make the best of them. Meditate on this card to improve your self-esteem or gain clarity about an issue.

20: Judgment

✦ In questions about money

You must make a choice regarding a money matter. This choice could take you away from the path you've been following and change your life. Your decision will affect not only your current situation, but also your finances in the future.

✦ In questions about love

You are facing a time of decision regarding a relationship. Issues of power, ethics, and honesty may be involved. Weigh your choice seriously—it could profoundly affect your association with a current partner as well as how you relate to others in the future.

✦ In questions about work

A major decision about your job or career path is necessary. It may be time to change jobs or find an altogether different line of work. What you do now will have long-term, far-reaching implications, so choose carefully.

✦ As a person you know

This card can represent someone who is in a position to pass judgment or make decisions for others, such as a judge, elected official, or other authority figure. Judgment may also symbolize a person who serves as a catalyst for change.

✦ As a card for personal growth

Judgment symbolizes a time of transition and the end of a cycle in your personal development. Assess your actions, beliefs, and progress before you decide how to proceed in the future. A major change might be necessary—meditating on this card can help you determine which path to take.

21: The World

✦ **In questions about money**

Financial matters are developing according to plan and everything is as it should be. An investment or monetary venture will come to fruition at its own speed—you can't rush it. Thoroughness is important. You'll reap the rewards you deserve.

✦ **In questions about love**

A relationship is developing at a slow, steady pace. You are in harmony with the times, so relax and don't try to force something to happen prematurely. Everything you've learned about love thus far plays a role in this partnership. This card symbolizes fulfillment and emotional maturity. It can also show a relationship evolving from a purely personal level to a spiritual one.

✦ In questions about work

Your goals can be achieved because they are in sync with the times. Everything is going according to plan, even though it may seem to be taking longer than you had hoped. Pay attention to details and use the knowledge and skills you've learned in the past to achieve a positive result.

✦ As a person you know

The World may symbolize someone who doesn't have to struggle to achieve happiness or success. This individual works *with* the forces of the Universe rather than against them. By using his or her abilities wisely, this person makes slow, steady progress in life.

✦ As a card for personal growth

You have learned life's lessons well and are exactly where you should be in your personal development. Continue growing in this slow, steady manner. All is right with the world at this time.

Index

Resources

Alexander, Skye. *10-Minute Crystal Ball.* Gloucester, Mass.:
    Fair Winds Press, 2002.

Alexander, Skye. *10-Minute Feng Shui.* Gloucester, Mass.:
    Fair Winds Press, 2002.

Alexander, Skye. *10-Minute Magic Spells.* Gloucester, Mass.:
    Fair Winds Press, 2003.

Alexander, Skye. *Magickal Astrology.* Franklin Lakes, N.J.:
    New Page Books, 2000.

Bluestone, Sarvananda. *How to Read Signs and Omens in Everyday
    Life.* Rochester, Vt.: Destiny Books/Inner Traditions, 2002.

Kaplan, Stuart. *Encyclopedia of the Tarot.* Stamford, Conn.:
    U.S. Games Systems, Inc. (Three volumes), 2003.

Conway, D. J., Sirona Knight, and Lisa Hunt. *Shapeshifter Tarot.*
    St. Paul, Minn.: Llewellyn Publications, 1998.

Franklin, Anna, and Mason, Paul. *The Sacred Circle Tarot.*
    St. Paul, Minn.: Llewellyn Publications, 1998.

Mann, A. T. *The Elements of the Tarot.* Shaftesbury, England:
    Element Books, 1993.

Williams, Brian. *The Minchiate Tarot.* Rochester, Vt.:
    Destiny Books/Inner Traditions, 1999.

About the Author

Skye Alexander is the author of *10-Minute Feng Shui, 10-Minute Crystal Ball, 10-Minute Magic Spells,* two astrology books—*Magickal Astrology* and *Planets in Signs*—and the mystery novel *Hidden Agenda,* which won the 1998 Kiss of Death Award for the year's best book of romantic suspense. A contributing author to *Your Birthday Sign through Time, The Big Book of Love, A Taste of Murder,* and *A Witch Like Me,* she has also written for numerous magazines, newspapers, TV, and radio. Her stories have been published in literary magazines and included in the anthologies *Mystery in Mind, Making Love on Cape Ann,* and *AstroMysteries.* She lives in Massachusetts with her cat, Domino.